CHRISTMAS
TREATS

Brighten your Christmas parties

GUILLAUME MARINETTE

PHOTOGRAPHS BY SANDRA MAHUT

TRANSLATED BY HOWARD CURTIS

CHRISTMAS TREATS

50 SWEET RECIPES FOR THE FESTIVE SEASON

OH EDITIONS

CONTENTS

Sweet Treats p. 6

Cookies and Biscuits p. 20

Cakes and Desserts p. 50

Yuletide Logs p. 72

Breads and Pastries p. 90

Drinks and Cocktails p. 102

Christmas Truffles

 Makes 15

 Preparation time
10 minutes
Refrigeration time
2 hours

Ingredients
250 g (9 oz) dark (bittersweet) chocolate
100 ml (3 ½ fl oz/scant ½ cup) double (heavy) cream
20 g (¾ oz/4 tsp) butter, at room temperature
100 g (3 ½ oz/1 ¾ cups) unsweetened cocoa powder

Specialist equipment
Bain-marie
Balloon (wire) whisk

- Finely chop the chocolate, place in a bowl and melt it in a bain-marie or microwave. When it is fully melted remove it from the heat.

- Gently warm the cream in a small pan and pour into the bowl with the melted chocolate. Add the softened butter and mix together using a balloon whisk until the mixture is smooth. Cover the bowl with clingfilm (plastic wrap) and leave in the refrigerator for 2 hours to set.

- Remove the truffle mixture from the refrigerator and use a teaspoon to scoop out a small amount into the palm of your hand. Roll between your palms to make 15 small balls.

- Place the cocoa powder in a shallow bowl and roll the truffles in the powder until fully coated.

You can vary this recipe by using flavoured chocolate, if you prefer.

 Yummy tip

To roll the truffles more easily, wash your hands regularly and dry them well.

Mendiants

 Makes 15

 Preparation time
10 minutes

 Ingredients
150 g (5 oz) dark (bittersweet)
chocolate
2 tbsp candied orange peel
2 tbsp shelled pistachios
2 tbsp shelled almonds
2 tbsp roasted hazelnuts
(filberts)

Specialist equipment
Bain-marie

- Finely chop the chocolate, place in a bowl and melt it in a bain-marie or microwave. When it is fully melted remove it from the heat.

- Place 1 tablespoon of the melted chocolate on a sheet of baking parchment and spread the chocolate thinly to form a disc. Repeat this until you have 15 discs and all the chocolate has been used.

- Sprinkle pieces of the candied orange peel and some nuts on each mendiant.

- Leave to set in a cool dry place.

You can vary this recipe by using flavoured chocolate, if you prefer.

 *Yummy tip*

To make the chocolate glossier, add 3 squares of chocolate to the melted chocolate and mix until the squares have fully melted.

Marzipan Dates

 Makes 15

 Preparation time
10 minutes

 Ingredients
15 Medjool dates
1 tbsp orange blossom water
150 g (5 oz) marzipan
(sugared almond paste),
whichever colour you prefer
2 tbsp caster (superfine)
sugar

Specialist equipment
Pastry brush

- Using a small sharp knife, split the dates on one side and remove the stone. Use a pastry brush to brush the bottom of each date with the orange blossom water.

- Cut the marzipan into 15 cubes and roll each cube with the palm of your hand to make small cylindrical pieces the same length as the dates. Place a piece of marzipan inside each date.

- Place the sugar in a shallow bowl and roll the filled dates in the sugar to give them a frosted effect.

These dates are dressed to kill!

Yummy tip

Use fresh not dried dates: they are better. Dried dates will be too sweet for this recipe.

Soft Nougat

Makes 50 pieces

Preparation time
50 minutes
Resting time
Overnight

Ingredients
120 g (4 oz/¾ cup) shelled almonds
95 g (3 ½ oz/⅔ cup) shelled hazelnuts (filberts)
35 g (1 ¼ oz/¼ cup) shelled pistachios
2 egg whites
175 g (6 oz/½ cup) glucose (corn) syrup
100 g (3 ½ oz/generous ¼ cup) honey
400 g (14 oz/2 cups) caster (superfine) sugar
Flavourings: vanilla, violet, tonka bean (optional)
Sheets of rice paper

Specialist equipment
Heatproof bowl
Sugar thermometer
Large pan or bain-marie

- Preheat the oven to 180°C (350°F/Gas Mark 4).

- Spread the nuts on a baking tray lined with baking parchment and roast in the preheated oven for 10 minutes, keeping an eye on them to ensure they don't burn. Set aside to cool.

- Place the egg whites in a clean heatproof bowl and beat with an electric whisk until stiff peaks form.

- Heat the glucose syrup, honey, sugar and 120 ml/4 fl oz/ ½ cup of water in a pan until the temperature reaches 143°C (290°F) on a sugar thermometer. It is important for the mix to reach this temperature to ensure the recipe is successful.

- Begin whisking the egg whites again and slowly drizzle the hot syrup mixture into them, whisking continuously. Add flavourings of your choice, if using. The mixture will thicken and turn yellow.

- Place the heatproof bowl over a pan of simmering water or use a bain-marie and stir the mixture continuously with a wooden spoon to dry it out. After about 25 minutes the mixture should start to come away from the bowl and will be ready. If you want a harder nougat, continue heating and stirring for a few minutes more.

- Remove the bowl from the heat, add the roasted nuts and mix well until fully incorporated.

- Pour the mixture out onto a sheet of rice paper and smooth the surface well with a spatula. Cover with another sheet of rice paper and leave overnight in a cool, dry place to set.

- Cut up the nougat into 50 bite-sized pieces with a sharp knife.

- Placed in a cellophane bag with a ribbon, these make a beautiful Christmas gift for friends or family.

Dark Chocolate Orangettes

 Makes 25

 Preparation time
10 minutes

 Ingredients
150 g (5 oz) dark (bittersweet) chocolate
25 slices candied orange

Specialist equipment
Bain-marie

- Finely chop the chocolate, place in a bowl and melt it in a bain-marie or microwave. When it is fully melted remove it from the heat.

- One at a time, dip each slice of candied orange in the melted chocolate to cover half of it in the chocolate and place on a sheet of baking parchment.

- Leave the orangettes in a cool dry place to set.

A taste of happiness …

Yummy tip

To make the chocolate glossier, add 3 squares of chocolate to the melted chocolate and mix until the squares have fully melted.

Santa's Hat Meringues

 Makes 12

 Preparation time
20 minutes
Cooking time
1 hour

 Ingredients
4 egg whites
250 g (9 oz/generous 1 cup)
caster (superfine) sugar
50 g (2 oz/generous ½ cup)
desiccated coconut
Red food colouring

Specialist equipment
2 piping (pastry) bags
1 large (12 mm) star
nozzle (tip)
1 (10 mm) smooth
nozzle (tip)

- Preheat the oven to 90°C (195°F/Gas Mark ¼).

- Place the egg whites in a clean bowl and beat with an electric whisk. Gradually mix in the sugar, whisking continuously, until stiff, glossy peaks form.

- Place half the meringue mix in a separate bowl and add half the desiccated coconut. Gently fold in the coconut using a silicone spatula, taking care not to deflate the meringue. Add a few drops of red food colouring to the other half of the meringue mix and gently fold to incorporate.

- Fill a piping bag, fitted with a star nozzle, with the red meringue mix. Fit the other piping bag with the smooth nozzle and fill with the coconut meringue mix.

- Cover a baking sheet with baking parchment and pipe 12 discs of white meringue onto the paper, each measuring about 2.5 cm (1 inch) in diameter. Sprinkle with the remaining coconut. Next, pipe the red meringue mix on top of each white disc to form the conical shape of Santa's hat, ensuring the base of the hat is wider and it tapers at the top.

- Finish off each hat with a little ball of piped white meringue to make the pompom. It is a little fiddly but you can add a little coconut to the pompom, if you like.

- Bake in the preheated oven for an hour then turn off the oven and leave the meringues inside to cool with the door left ajar.

- When the meringues are completely cool, remove from the oven and peel them from the baking parchment.

These irresistible hats are best kept in a tin or airtight container.

Melted Snowmen

 Makes 20

Preparation time
10 minutes

Ingredients
200 g (7 oz) bar white chocolate
40 edible sugar eyes
60 red Skittles®
10 straight pretzels
20 orange jellybeans
2 bars Toblerone®

Specialist equipment
Bain-marie
Silicone mat or a sheet of baking parchment

- Finely chop the white chocolate, place in a bowl and melt it in a bain-marie or microwave. Pour the melted chocolate onto a silicone mat or a sheet of baking parchment to form a thin layer.

- Working quickly, make the snowmen while the chocolate is still very soft. Stick on the eyes, use the red Skittles® for buttons, form the arms with the pretzels; for the nose, cut the jelly beans in half; and for the hat, place a piece of Toblerone®. Repeat until you have 20 snowmen.

- Use a knife or cocktail stick to score the outline of each snowman in the chocolate as it begins to set but is still soft. Set aside to set completely.

- Once the chocolate has set, carefully peel each snowman from the mat or paper. The chocolate will break along the score lines.

A snowman that melts in the mouth!

 *Yummy tip*

You can have fun making lots of different snowmen. Vary the sweets and use your imagination!

Christmas Stars

Makes 20 biscuits

Preparation time
10 minutes, plus extra
to decorate
Cooking time
10 minutes

Ingredients
175 g (6 oz/scant ½ cup) plain
(all-purpose) flour
80 g (3 oz/½ cup) brown
sugar
1 tsp allspice
60 g (2 oz) butter, at room
temperature
3 tbsp whole (full-fat) milk
1 egg yolk
Royal icing (frosting)
1 egg white
250 g (9 oz/2 cups) icing
(confectioners') sugar
Food colouring, in your
preferred colours (optional)
Sugar sprinkles or
decorations

Specialist equipment
Rolling pin
5 cm (2 inch) star-shaped
pastry cutter

- Preheat the oven to 110°C (230°F/Gas Mark ¼).

- Mix the flour, brown sugar and allspice in a mixing bowl. Add the softened butter and knead the mixture with your fingers until the texture is grainy. Add the milk and egg yolk and mix well until you have a smooth, uniform dough.

- Roll out the dough to a thickness of 6 mm (¼ inch) on a lightly floured worktop. Use the pastry cutter to cut out roughly 20 star-shaped biscuits (cookies) from the dough.

- Arrange the biscuits on a baking sheet lined with baking parchment, leaving 1 cm (½ inch) between each biscuit to allow for them to spread.

- Bake in the preheated oven for 10 minutes. Remove from the oven and set aside to cool for 5 minutes before transferring to a wire cooling rack to cool completely.

- For the royal icing place the egg white in a clean bowl and start to beat with an electric whisk on low speed, adding the icing sugar a little at a time. Continue to beat the mix until the sugar has been fully incorporated and you obtain a smooth thick mixture.

- If you wish to use coloured icing divide the mixture evenly into separate bowls for each colour. Add a few drops of food colouring to the icing and mix until you achieve the desired colour. Cover each bowl with clingfilm (plastic wrap) to prevent the icing from drying out when not in use.

- Decorate the biscuits.

You can add sprinkles, sugar strands, pearls or dragees in whichever colours you prefer, or sprinkle with granulated sugar to give a snow effect.

Christmas Spice Fondant

 Makes 16

 Preparation time
10 minutes
Cooking time
25 minutes

 Ingredients
140 g (5 oz) butter, at room temperature
125 g (4 oz/⅔ cup) brown sugar
50 g (2 oz/¼ cup) caster (superfine) sugar
1 egg + 1 yolk
190 g (6 ¾ oz/1 ⅔ cups) plain (all-purpose) flour
1 ½ tsp allspice
1 tsp baking powder
75 g (2 ½ oz) bar white chocolate
75 g (2 ½ oz) bar milk chocolate

Specialist equipment
Square cake tin (pan) with 20–22cm (8–9 inch) sides

- Preheat the oven to 180°C (350°F/Gas Mark 4).

- Using an electric whisk, beat the butter with the sugars in a mixing bowl until the mixture is pale and fluffy. Add the whole egg and the yolk and continue to whisk until fully incorporated.

- In a separate bowl, mix together the flour, allspice and baking powder. Gradually add the dry ingredients to the butter and sugar mix, beating continuously until combined.

- Cut the chocolate bars into small chunks and add them to the mixture.

- Pour the mixture into a cake tin lined with baking parchment and bake in the preheated oven for 25 minutes.

- Leave to cool in the tin before removing and cutting into 16 squares.

Enjoy with coffee for a perfect pick-me-up.

Yummy tip

Store these in an airtight container to keep them moist.

Hanging Heart Biscuits

 Makes 30

 Preparation time
15 minutes plus decorating
Cooking time
6–8 minutes
Resting time
2 hours

 Ingredients
4 egg yolks
125 g (4 oz/generous ½ cup) caster (superfine) sugar
125 g (4 oz) butter, at room temperature
½ tsp vanilla powder or the grated zest of 1 lemon
250 g (9 oz/2 cups) plain (all-purpose) flour
Royal icing
1 egg white
250 g (9 oz/2 cups) icing (confectioners') sugar
Food colouring, in your preferred colours (optional)

Specialist equipment
5 cm (2 inch) heart-shaped pastry cutter
String

- Using an electric whisk, beat the egg yolks with the caster (superfine) sugar in a mixing bowl until the mixture turns white. Add the butter and vanilla (or lemon zest) and keep whisking until the mixture is pale and fluffy, then add the flour and mix well until you have a smooth, uniform dough. Shape the dough into a ball and leave in a cool place for 2 hours, wrapped in clingfilm (plastic wrap).

- Preheat the oven to 160°C (320°F/Gas Mark 2).

- Roll out the dough to a thickness of 5 mm (¼ inch) on a lightly floured worktop or between 2 sheets of baking parchment. Use the pastry cutter or a knife to cut out 30 heart-shaped biscuits from the dough.

- Arrange the biscuits on a baking sheet lined with baking parchment, leaving 1 cm (½ inch) between each biscuit to allow for them to spread. Using a straw, pierce a small hole in the biscuits so that you can hang them on a string.

- Bake in the preheated oven for 6–8 minutes then remove from the oven and leave to cool for 5 minutes before transferring to a wire cooling rack to cool completely.

- For the royal icing, place the egg white in a clean bowl and start to beat with an electric whisk on low speed, adding the icing sugar a little at a time. Continue to beat the mix until the sugar has been fully incorporated and you have a smooth, thick mixture.

- Decorate the biscuits.

You can vary the taste of these biscuits by flavouring the dough with lime zest or cinnamon instead of the vanilla powder or lemon zest.

Honey Reindeer Biscuits

 Makes 10–30 biscuits, depending on size

 Preparation time
10 minutes
Cooking time
10–12 minutes
Resting time
30 minutes

Ingredients
250 g (9 oz/2 cups) plain (all-purpose) flour
130 g (4 oz) butter, at room temperature
80 g (3 oz/⅓ cup) caster (superfine) sugar
2 egg yolks
3 tbsp honey
Grated zest of 1 lemon

Specialist equipment
Rolling pin
Reindeer-shaped pastry cutter

- Place the flour in a large mixing bowl and make a well in the centre. Place all the other ingredients in the well and gently knead everything together to form a smooth, uniform dough.

- Shape the dough into a ball and leave in a cool place for 30 minutes, wrapped in clingfilm (plastic wrap).

- Preheat the oven to 150°C (300°F/Gas Mark 1).

- Roll out the dough to a thickness of 5 mm (¼ inch) on a lightly floured worktop or between 2 sheets of baking parchment. Use the pastry cutter to cut out roughly 20 reindeers from the dough.

- Arrange the biscuits on a baking sheet lined with baking parchment, leaving 1 cm (½ inch) between each biscuit to allow for them to spread.

- Bake in the preheated oven for 10–12 minutes then remove from the oven and leave to cool for 5 minutes before transferring to a wire cooling rack to cool completely.

The perfect cookies to leave out for Santa.

Yummy tip

You can decorate these biscuits with royal icing, if you like (see page 24).

Speculoos

 Makes 30

 Preparation time
20 minutes
Cooking time
20 minutes
Resting time
12 hours + 2 hours cooling

 Ingredients
150 g (5 oz/1 ¼ cups) plain
(all-purpose) flour
½ tsp bicarbonate of soda
(baking soda)
pinch of salt
1 ½ tsp allspice
125 g (4 oz/⅔ cup)
muscovado sugar
50 g (2 oz) butter, melted
1 tbsp Cointreau® (optional)

Specialist equipment
Pastry cutter

- Mix the flour with the bicarbonate of soda, salt, allspice and sugar in a mixing bowl (you can adjust the spiciness by decreasing or increasing the allspice, according to your taste). Pour the melted butter over the dry ingredients and stir gently with a wooden spoon to combine.

- Add the Cointreau®, if using. For a perfectly smooth dough, gently add a little warm water until the dough is slightly sticky.

- Shape the dough into a ball and leave in a cool place for 12 hours, wrapped in clingfilm (plastic wrap).

- Preheat the oven to 160°C (320°F/Gas Mark 2).

- Roll out the dough to a thickness of 3–4 mm (¼–⅛ inch) on a lightly floured worktop. Use the pastry cutter or a knife to cut out 30 biscuits from the dough.

- Arrange the biscuits on a baking sheet lined with baking parchment, leaving 1 cm (½ inch) between each biscuit to allow for them to spread.

- Bake in the preheated oven for 20 minutes. The biscuits must be well baked in order to be crisp.

- Remove from the oven and leave to cool for 5 minutes before transferring to a wire cooling rack to cool for at least 2 hours before eating.

The perfect Christmas biscuit!

Yummy tip

Don't hesitate to add patterns and shapes using a patterned rolling pin!

Shortbread Stars

 Makes 20

 Preparation time
10 minutes
Cooking time
30 minutes

 Ingredients
300 g (10 ½ oz/2 ½ cups)
plain (all-purpose) flour
200 g (7 oz) slightly salted
butter, at room temperature
100 g (3 ½ oz/scant ½ cup)
caster (superfine) sugar
50 g (2 oz) candied fruits, cut
into small cubes

Specialist equipment
Rolling pin
5 cm (2 in) star-shaped pastry
cutter
Metal skewer

- Preheat the oven to 150°C (300°F/Gas Mark 1).

- Mix the flour and softened butter together in a bowl, kneading well with your fingers. Add the sugar and candied fruits, and continue kneading carefully until you have a smooth, uniform dough.

- Roll out the dough to a thickness of 1 cm (½ inch) on a lightly floured worktop or between 2 sheets of baking parchment. Use the pastry cutter or a knife to cut out 20 star-shaped biscuits from the dough.

- Arrange the biscuits on a baking sheet lined with baking parchment, leaving 1 cm (½ inch) between each biscuit to allow for them to spread. Prick the surface of each shortbread evenly all over with a skewer.

- Bake in the preheated oven for 30 minutes then remove from the oven and leave to cool for 5 minutes before transferring to a wire cooling rack to cool completely before eating or storing in an airtight container.

A very British Christmas!

Yummy tip

You can experiment with the taste of these biscuits by replacing the candied fruits with the zest of citrus fruits or chocolate chips.

Gingerbread Men

 Makes 20

 Preparation time
15 minutes
Cooking time
10 minutes
Resting time
1 hour

Ingredients
1 egg
80 g (3 oz/scant ½ cup)
brown sugar
50 g (2 oz/¼ cup) caster
(superfine) sugar
50 g (2 oz/7 tsp) honey
130 g (4 oz) butter, melted
280 g (10 oz/2 ⅓ cups) plain
(all-purpose) flour
2 tbsp cinnamon
1 tbsp ground ginger
½ tsp nutmeg
½ tsp ground aniseed
pinch of bicarbonate of soda
(baking soda)
1 tsp vanilla extract
pinch of salt

**For the royal icing (frosting)
ingredients see page 24**

Specialist equipment
9 cm (3.5 inch) gingerbread
man-shaped pastry cutter

- Using an electric whisk, beat the egg with the brown and caster sugars, honey and melted butter in a mixing bowl. Add the flour, spices, bicarbonate of soda vanilla and salt, and knead together until you have a smooth, uniform dough. Shape the dough into 2 equal-sized balls and leave in a cool place for 1 hour, wrapped in clingfilm (plastic wrap).

- Preheat the oven to 180°C (350°F/Gas Mark 4).

- Roll out the dough to a thickness of 3–4 mm (¼–⅛ inch) on a lightly floured worktop or between 2 sheets of baking parchment. Use the pastry cutter to cut out 20 gingerbread men from the dough. Arrange the biscuits (cookies) on a baking sheet lined with baking parchment, leaving 1 cm (½ inch) between each biscuit to allow for them to spread.

- Bake in the preheated oven for about 10 minutes then remove from the oven and leave to cool for 5 minutes before transferring to a wire cooling rack to cool completely.

- For the royal icing method, see page 24. If you wish to use coloured icing, divide the mixture evenly into separate bowls for each colour. Add a few drops of food colouring to the icing and mix until you achieve the desired colour. Cover each bowl with clingfilm to prevent the icing from drying out when not in use.

- Decorate the biscuits. Get creative! You can draw whatever clothing you'd like with icing, or add sweets or chocolate chips.

 *Yummy
tip*

You can freeze the raw biscuits and use them throughout the holiday period.

Christmas Crescents

Makes 40

Preparation time
10 minutes
Cooking time
15 minutes

Ingredients
1 vanilla pod (bean)
35 g (1 ¼ oz/3 tbsp) caster (superfine) sugar
125 g (4 oz) butter, at room temperature
140 g (5 oz/generous 1 cup) plain (all-purpose) flour
60 g (2 oz/generous ½ cup) ground almonds
30 g (1 oz) crystallised orange peel, cut into cubes (optional)
60 g (2 oz/½ cup) icing (confectioners') sugar, for decoration

- Preheat the oven to 170°C (340°F/Gas Mark 3).

- Remove the seeds from the vanilla pod and mix with the caster sugar in a mixing bowl. Add the remaining ingredients except the icing sugar and knead together until you have a smooth, uniform dough.

- Divide the dough into 4 equal parts and, using your palms, roll each piece of dough into a cylinder about 20 cm (8 inches) long. Cut each cylinder at 2 cm (¾ inch) intervals to give 10 equal-sized pieces. Roll each piece into a small cylinder and curl it around into the shape of a crescent moon.

- Arrange the crescents on a baking sheet lined with baking parchment, leaving 1 cm (½ inch) between each biscuit to allow for them to spread.

- Bake in the preheated oven for about 15 minutes then remove from the oven and leave to cool for 5 minutes before transferring to a wire cooling rack to cool completely.

- When the biscuits have cooled, roll them in the icing sugar.

I melt in the mouth!

Yummy tip

You can vary the taste of these biscuits with candied fruits of your choice.

Saint Nicolas' Walking Sticks

Makes 60

Preparation time
25 minutes
Cooking time
15–20 minutes
Resting time
30 minutes

Ingredients
260 g (9 oz) butter, at room temperature
150 g (5 oz/1 ¼ cups) icing (confectioners') sugar
120 ml (4 fl oz/½ cup) whole (full-fat) milk, at room temperature
1 tbsp vanilla extract
380 g (13 oz/2 ¼ cups) plain (all-purpose) flour
Decoration
80g (3 oz) bar dark (bittersweet) chocolate
Sugar sprinkles, hundreds and thousands

Specialist equipment
Piping (pastry) bag
10 mm star nozzle (tip)
Bain-marie

• Using a silicone spatula, mix the softened butter and icing sugar together in a mixing bowl until it has a creamy texture. Add the milk and vanilla extract and mix to combine. When the mixture is of a uniform consistency, spread it out on a worktop to a thickness of 1 cm (½ inch). Add the flour and carefully knead until the flour is fully incorporated and you have a smooth uniform dough. Take care not to overwork the dough.

• Fit a piping bag with a 10 mm star nozzle and fill with the dough. Line a baking sheet with baking parchment and pipe the dough onto the paper in the shape of a 2 cm (1 inch) walking stick. Repeat until all the dough is used up, leaving a small space between each stick to allow for them to spread; you should have about 60 sticks. Set aside for 30 minutes to form a crust so that the biscuits (cookies) do not spread during baking.

• Preheat the oven to 180°C (350°F/Gas Mark 4).

• Bake in the preheated oven for 15–20 minutes then remove from the oven and leave to cool for 5 minutes before transferring to a wire cooling rack to cool completely.

• Finely chop the chocolate, place in a bowl and melt it in a bain-marie or microwave. When it is fully melted remove it from the heat.

• When the walking sticks have cooled, dip the lower half of each biscuit in the melted chocolate, placing each on a sheet of baking parchment as you work. Sprinkle the hundreds and thousands on the chocolate while it is still soft and leave to set in a dry, well-ventilated place.

• Keep the biscuits in a tin or airtight container.

You can dip these in white, milk or dark chocolate.

Little Teddy Bears

 Makes 20

 Preparation time
15 minutes
Cooking time
15 minutes
Resting time
1 hour + 30 minutes

 Ingredients
120 g (4 oz/ 1 cup) plain (all-purpose) flour
60 g (2 oz) butter
50 g (2 oz/scant ½ cup) icing (confectioners') sugar
20 g (¾ oz/¼ cup) ground almonds
20 g (¾ oz/¼ cup) ground pistachios
1 tsp unsweetened cocoa
1 egg
10 whole almonds
10 pistachios

Specialist equipment
Stand mixer fitted with a flat beater attachment
4 cm (1½ inch) teddy bear-shaped pastry cutter

- Place all the ingredients except the egg, whole almonds and pistachios together in the bowl of a stand mixer with a flat beater attached and mix to combine until the mixture has a grainy texture. Add the egg and continue mixing until incorporated and you have a smooth, uniform dough. Shape the dough into a ball and leave in a cool place for 1 hour, wrapped in clingfilm (plastic wrap)

- Roll out the dough to a thickness of 4 mm (¼ inch) on a lightly floured worktop or between 2 sheets of baking parchment. Use the pastry cutter to cut out 20 teddy bears from the dough.

- Arrange the biscuits on a baking sheet lined with baking parchment, leaving 1 cm (½ inch) between each biscuit to allow for them to spread. Place an almond or a pistachio on the middle of each of the teddy bears and fold the bear's arms around the nut. Set aside in a cool place for 30 minutes.

- Preheat the oven to 180°C (350°F/ Gas Mark 4).

- Bake in the preheated oven for about 15 minutes then remove from the oven and leave to cool for 5 minutes before transferring to a wire cooling rack to cool completely.

Really cute and really delicious!

 *Yummy tip*

Vary the nuts: use almonds, walnuts or pecans, if you prefer.

Vanilla and Chocolate Whirls

Makes 30 (depending on thickness)

Preparation time
20 minutes
Resting time
45 minutes
Freezing time
30 minutes
Cooking time
20 minutes

Ingredients
450 g (1 lb/3 ¾ cups) plain (all-purpose) flour
200 g (7 oz/scant 1 cup) caster (superfine) sugar
11 g (1 ½ sachets/ 1 tsp) vanilla sugar
pinch of fleur de sel
270 g (10 oz) butter, at room temperature
2 egg whites
15 g (½ oz/2 tbsp) unsweetened cocoa powder

Specialist equipment
Pastry brush

- Place the flour, sugars and salt in a large mixing bowl. Cut the butter into small cubes and add to the bowl. Rub everything together using your fingertips to gradually incorporate all the flour into the butter until the mixture resembles breadcrumbs. Add 1 egg white and mix to combine until you have a smooth, uniform dough.

- Shape the dough into a ball and leave to rest under a clean tea (dish) towel, at room temperature, for 45 minutes.

- Divide the dough into 2 equal parts. Place one half in a separate bowl, add the cocoa powder and knead the dough until the cocoa is fully incorporated. Roll out each ball of dough between 2 sheets of baking parchment into rectangles, each 3 mm (¼–⅛ inch) thick and of the same size.

- Brush half the remaining egg white over the lighter-coloured rectangle of dough. Roll the darker-coloured rectangle around the rolling pin and place it on top of the vanilla dough rectangle. Brush the rest of the egg white over the chocolate dough rectangle. With the short edge of the rectangle towards you, roll the dough into a roulade, pressing down firmly as you roll. Place the roulade in the freezer for 30 minutes.

- Preheat the oven to 150°C (300°F/Gas Mark 1).

- Remove the roulade from the freezer and cut into slices. If you prefer a crunchy biscuit (cookie), cut the slices 5 mm (¼ inch) wide. For a more moist biscuit, cut the slices to a width of 1 cm (½ inch). Arrange the slices, flat side down, on a baking sheet lined with baking parchment, leaving 1 cm (½ inch) between each biscuit to allow for them to spread.

- Bake in the preheated oven for 20 minutes then remove from the oven and leave to cool for 5 minutes before transferring to a wire cooling rack to cool completely.

Jam Shortbread Bauble Biscuits

Makes 25

Preparation time
20 minutes
Cooking time
10 minutes
Resting time
30 minutes

Ingredients
200 g (7 oz) butter, at room temperature
200 g (7 oz/scant 1 cup) caster (superfine) sugar
16 g (2 sachets/4 tsp) vanilla sugar
2 eggs
500 g (1 lb 2 oz/4 cups) plain (all-purpose) flour
100 g (3 ½ oz/⅔ cup) ground hazelnuts (filberts)
100 g (3 ½ oz) strawberry jam (jelly)
20 g (¾ oz/7 tsp) icing (confectioners') sugar

Specialist equipment
Stand mixer fitted with a flat beater attachment
Bauble-shaped pastry cutters, or cutters of your choice
Small round pastry cutter about 2.5 cm (1 inch) in diameter

- Using a stand mixer with a flat beater attached, beat the butter with the caster and vanilla sugars in a mixing bowl until pale and fluffy. Add the eggs and mix to incorporate. Add the flour and ground hazelnuts and knead the mixture until you have a uniform dough.

- Shape the dough into a ball and leave in a cool place for 30 minutes.

- Preheat the oven to 150°C (300°F/Gas Mark 1).

- Roll out the dough to a thickness of 3–4 mm (¼–⅛ inch) on a lightly floured worktop or between 2 sheets of baking parchment. Use bauble-shaped pastry cutters, or cutters of your choice to cut out 25 biscuits (cookies) from the dough. Cut another 25 duplicate biscuits of the same shapes and sizes and, using a small round pastry cutter, cut a hole in the centre of these biscuits. Arrange all the biscuits on 2 baking sheets lined with baking parchment, leaving 1 cm (½ inch) between each biscuit to allow for them to spread.

- Bake in the preheated oven for 10 minutes, checking a few minutes before the end of the cooking time that the biscuits are not turning brown. Remove from the oven and leave to cool for 5 minutes before transferring to a wire cooling rack to cool completely.

- When the biscuits have cooled, spread the whole biscuits with the strawberry jam. Sprinkle the biscuits with the holes with icing sugar. Place the biscuits with holes on top of the whole biscuits to enclose the jam filling.

Yummy tip

Use different flavoured jams apricot, raspberry, fig, etc. or add sprinkles or edible glitter to the jam for a sparkly effect.

Crinkles

Makes about 16

Preparation time
25 minutes
Cooking time
11 minutes
Resting time
2 hours

Ingredients
200 g (7 oz) dark (bittersweet) chocolate
50 g (2 oz) butter
2 eggs
80 g (3 oz/scant ½ cup) brown sugar
8 g (1 sachet/2 tsp) vanilla sugar
210 g (7 ½ oz/scant 1 ¾ cups) plain (all-purpose) flour
30 g (1 oz) candied orange peel, cut into cubes
½ tsp baking powder
pinch of fleur de sel
30 g (1 oz/¼ cup) icing (confectioners') sugar

Specialist equipment
Bain-marie

- Finely chop the chocolate and place it in a bowl with the butter. Melt together in a bain-marie or microwave, stirring gently with a wooden spoon. When it is fully melted remove it from the heat.

- Using an electric whisk, beat the eggs with the brown and vanilla sugars in a mixing bowl until the mixture turns white. Add the melted chocolate, flour, candied orange peel, baking powder and salt, and mix together until you have a uniform dough.

- Shape the dough into a ball and leave in a cool place for 2 hours.

- Preheat the oven to 180°C (350°F/Gas Mark 4).

- Take small pieces of the dough and roll it between your palms to form about 16 walnut-sized balls. Place the icing sugar in a shallow bowl and roll the dough balls in the sugar.

- Arrange the balls on a baking sheet lined with baking parchment, leaving a 3 cm (1 ¼ inch) gap between each ball, as they will puff up and spread out as they cook.

- Bake in the preheated oven for 11 minutes. Remove from the oven and leave to cool for 5 minutes.

- Eat the crinkles while they are still warm or transfer to a wire cooling rack to cool completely.

Irresistible when they're still warm!

Yummy tip

Replace the candied orange with candied lemon, if you prefer.

Diamonds

 Makes 72

 Preparation time
15 minutes
Cooking time
15–18 minutes
Resting time
30 minutes

Ingredients
185 g (6 ½ oz) butter, at room temperature
100 g (3 ½ oz/generous ¾ cup) icing (confectioners') sugar
1 tbsp orange blossom water
2 g (1 tsp) salt
250 g (9 oz/2 cups) strong white (bread) flour
Decoration
50 g (2 oz/¼ cup) white granulated sugar
Silver sprinkles
1 egg white

Specialist equipment
Stand mixer fitted with a flat beater attachment
Pastry brush

- Place the softened butter and icing sugar in the bowl of a stand mixer with a flat beater attached and beat together until creamy. Add the orange blossom water and salt and continue beating to combine. Add the flour in one go, and mix on high speed until fully incorporated and you have a smooth, uniform dough.

- Divide the dough equally in half and roll each half into a cylinder 3 cm (1 ¼ inch) in diameter. Leave in a cool place for 30 minutes, wrapped in clingfilm (plastic wrap)

- Preheat the oven to 180°C (350°F/Gas Mark 4).

- Mix the granulated sugar and silver sprinkles together on a plate or tray. Brush each cylinder of dough with the egg white, then roll in the sugar/sprinkle mix until fully coated. Cut the cylinders into slices at least 1 cm (½ inch) wide.

- Arrange the slices, flat side down, on a baking sheet lined with baking parchment, leaving 3 cm (1 inch) between each biscuit to allow for them to spread.

- Bake in the preheated oven for 15–18 minutes, taking care not to overcook them. The diamonds should be slightly golden.

- Remove from the oven and leave to cool for 5 minutes before transferring to a wire cooling rack to cool completely. Store in a tin or airtight container.

Crunchy and delicious – a sparkly delight

Yummy tip

You can freeze the raw biscuits and bake them as and when you like.

Christmas Holly Biscuits

 Makes 20

 Preparation time
10 minutes
Cooking time
12 minutes
Resting time
1 hour

 Ingredients
2 eggs
200 g (7 oz/generous 1 cup) brown sugar
230 g (8 oz/1 ½ cups) wholemeal (whole-wheat) flour
150 g (5 oz/scant 1 ¼ cups) cornflour (cornstarch)
130 g (4 oz) butter
1 tsp baking powder
150 g (5 oz/1 cup) sesame seeds
1 tsp vanilla extract

For the royal icing (frosting) ingredients see page 24

Specialist equipment
Toothpick

- Using an electric whisk, beat the eggs with the brown sugar in a mixing bowl until the mixture turns pale and fluffy. Add all the remaining ingredients and mix together until you have a uniform dough.

- Shape the dough into a cylinder measuring 4 cm (1 ½ inches) in diameter and leave in a cool place for at least 1 hour, wrapped in a clean tea (dish) towel or clingfilm (plastic wrap).

- Preheat the oven to 210°C (410°F/Gas Mark 7).

- Cut the cylinder into slices about 1 cm (½ inch) wide – you should end up with 20 slices. Arrange the slices, flat side down, on a baking sheet lined with baking parchment, leaving 3 cm (1 ¼ inch) between each biscuit (cookie) to allow for them to spread.

- Bake in the preheated oven for 12 minutes then remove from the oven and leave to cool for 5 minutes before transferring to a wire cooling rack to cool completely.

- When the biscuits have cooled, make the royal icing using the method on page 24. Place a tablespoonful of the mix in 2 small bowls to use for the green and red icing. Add a drop of food colouring to the icing and mix until you achieve the desired colour. Cover each bowl with clingfilm to prevent the icing from drying out when not in use.

- Dip half of each biscuit in the white icing and place on a tray lined with baking parchment. While the icing is still soft, add a drop of the green icing and, with a toothpick, drag the icing out to form the spiky holly leaves. Add dots of the red icing to make the red holly berries.

You can also decorate the biscuits (cookies) with sugar pearls.

Christmas Bauble Cupcakes

Makes 12

Preparation time
30 minutes
Cooking time
20 minutes
Freezing time
4 hours

Ingredients
200 g (7 oz) dark (bittersweet) chocolate
200 g (7 oz) slightly salted butter, at room temperature
100 g (3 ½ oz/scant ½ cup) caster (superfine) sugar
4 eggs
120 g (4 oz/1 cup) self-raising (self-rising) flour
1 tbsp baking powder
Decoration
600 g (1 lb 5 oz) mascarpone
150 g (5 oz/1 ¼ cups) icing (confectioners') sugar
Food colouring, in your preferred colours (optional)
30 g (1 oz) fondant icing (sugar paste), coloured orange or gold

Specialist equipment
12-hole muffin tin (pan)
12 cupcake cases
Bain-marie
Silicone mould with 12 small spherical cavities
Piping (pastry) bag
10 mm star nozzle (tip)

- Preheat the oven to 180°C (350°F/Gas Mark 4) and line a 12-hole muffin tin with cases.

- Finely chop the chocolate and place it in a bowl with the butter. Melt together in a bain-marie or microwave, stirring gently with a wooden spoon. When it is fully melted remove it from the heat. Add the caster sugar to the melted chocolate and stir to combine. Add the eggs, one at a time, then the flour and baking powder. Mix together until fully incorporated and you have a uniform batter.

- Pour the batter into the cupcake cases until each is three quarters full and bake in the preheated oven for 20 minutes. Do not open the oven door until towards the end of the cooking time or the cakes may sink in the middle. The cakes are done when a skewer or toothpick inserted in the centre comes out clean and dry. Remove from the oven and leave to cool for 5 minutes before transferring to a wire cooling rack to cool completely.

- While the cakes are cooling, make the decoration. Using an electric whisk, beat the mascarpone and icing sugar together in a mixing bowl until you have quite a firm cream. If you like, you can divide the cream up at this stage and colour it with different food colourings.

- Fill a silicone mould that has 12 small spherical cavities with some of the mascarpone cream and place in the freezer for a minimum of 4 hours.

- Fit a piping bag with a star nozzle and fill with the remaining mascarpone cream. Pipe mascarpone cream around the edge of each cupcake to form a base for the frozen mascarpone ball to rest in.

- Remove a ball of frozen mascarpone cream from the silicone mould and place one on top of each cupcake. Finish by making a little looped hanger from the fondant icing and placing it on top of the bauble. Eat straight away, while still cold.

Fir Tree Cupcakes

Makes 12

Preparation time
20 minutes
Cooking time
20 minutes

Ingredients
120 g (4 oz) slightly salted butter
2 eggs
120 g (4 oz/generous ½ cup) caster (superfine) sugar
120 g (4 oz/1 cup) self-raising (self-rising) flour
Decoration
600 g (1 lb 5 oz) mascarpone
150 g (5 oz/1 ¼ cups) icing (confectioners') sugar
Whipping cream
Green food colouring
Sugar pearls, sprinkles or edible glitter

Specialist equipment
12-hole muffin tin (pan)
12 cupcake cases
Piping (pastry) bag
8–10 mm star nozzle (tip)

- Preheat the oven to 180°C (350°F/Gas Mark 4) and line a 12-hole muffin tin with cases.

- Melt the butter in a microwave or small saucepan. Using an electric whisk, beat the eggs with the caster sugar in a mixing bowl until the mixture doubles in size. Stop whisking and fold in the flour a tablespoon at a time then stir in the melted butter until you have a uniform batter.

- Pour the batter into the cupcake cases until each is three quarters full and bake in the preheated oven for 20 minutes. Do not open the oven door until towards the end of the cooking time or the cakes may sink in the middle. The cakes are done when a skewer or toothpick inserted in the centre comes out clean and dry.

- Remove from the oven and leave to cool for 5 minutes before transferring to a wire cooling rack to cool completely before decorating.

- Using an electric whisk, beat the mascarpone, icing sugar and cream together to just combine. Add a few drops of the green food colouring and continue whisking until you have quite a firm whipped cream.

- Fit a piping bag with a star nozzle and fill with the green mascarpone cream. Pipe the cream on top of the muffins in one continuous swirl, starting from the outer edge and tapering upwards into the shape of a fir tree.

- Decorate with sugar pearls, sprinkles or edible glitter. Eat straight away.

These are sure to impress – and taste delicious!

Frozen Nougat with Coulis

 Serves 6

 Preparation time
50 minutes
Freezing time
12 hours

 Ingredients
100 g (3 ½ oz/1 cup) shelled almonds
50 g (2 oz/generous cup) shelled hazelnuts (filberts)
75 g (2 ½ oz/½ cup) shelled pistachios
110 g (3 ¾ oz/½ cup) white caster (superfine) sugar
3 eggs
100 g (3 ½ oz/generous ¼ cup) honey
400 ml (13 fl oz/generous 1 ½ cups) whipping cream, chilled
150 ml (5 fl oz/⅔ scant cup) red fruit coulis, to serve

Specialist equipment
Baking tray (pan)
10 x 4 cm (4 x 1 ¾ inch) silicone mould

- Preheat the oven to 180°C (350°F/Gas Mark 4).

- Spread the nuts on a baking tray lined with baking parchment. Sprinkle over a tablespoon of the sugar and roast in the preheated oven for 10 minutes. Set aside to cool.

- Break the eggs and separate the whites from the yolks. Place the egg whites in a clean bowl and beat with an electric whisk until stiff peaks form. Boil the honey in a small saucepan then begin whisking the egg whites again and slowly drizzle the hot honey into them, whisking continuously. Set aside.

- In a separate bowl, whisk the egg yolks with the remaining sugar until the mixture turns white. Gently fold in the whisked egg whites, taking care not to deflate the mixture.

- Whip the cream until it is quite firm and carefully fold into the whisked egg whites, then fold in the roasted nuts. Pour the mixture into a silicone mould and place in the freezer for 12 hours.

- Remove from the mould and place the frozen nougat on 6 individual dessert plates, and drizzle the red fruit coulis over the top.

A refreshing take on a traditional sweet-shop favourite.

Yummy tip

Change the nuts according to your taste – or you could add dried or candied fruits instead.

Snowman Tiramisu

 Serves 6

 Preparation time
20 minutes
Resting time
3 hours

Ingredients
3 eggs
100 g (3 ½ oz/scant ½ cup)
caster (superfine) sugar
250 g (9 oz) mascarpone
200 ml (7 fl oz/scant
1 cup) strong coffee
4 tbsp amaretto
20 soft chocolate biscuits
(cookies)
Decoration
200 ml (7 fl oz/scant 1 cup)
whipping cream, chilled
20 g (¾ oz/scant ¼ cup) icing
(confectioners') sugar
6 white marshmallows
30 g (1 oz) milk or dark
(bittersweet) chocolate,
melted
6 orange jelly beans
Strawberry lace sweets
(candies)

Specialist equipment
6 short glass tumblers
Piping (pastry) bag
10 cm (4 inch) smooth
nozzle (tip)

- Break the eggs and separate the whites from the yolks. Using an electric whisk, beat the yolks with the caster sugar in a mixing bowl until the mixture is pale and fluffy. Add the mascarpone and continue to whisk until fully incorporated with a smooth uniform texture.

- Place the egg whites in a clean bowl and beat with an electric whisk until stiff peaks form. Gently fold the whisked egg whites into the mascarpone mixture, taking care not to deflate it.

- Pour the coffee with the amaretto into a shallow bowl, then, one by one, dip the chocolate biscuits in the coffee mix and place in the bottom of 6 short glass tumblers. You may need to cut the biscuits to fit the glasses; do this before soaking the biscuits in the coffee. Take care not to soak the biscuits too much or they will become too soft. When you have a layer of biscuits at the bottom of each glass, cover it generously with the mascarpone. Repeat the layers until all the biscuits and mascarpone mixture has been used. Leave to stand in a cool place for 3 hours.

- Using an electric whisk, whip the cream and icing sugar together in a mixing bowl until you have a firm whipped cream. Fit a piping bag with a smooth nozzle and fill the bag with the whipped cream. Pipe the cream on top of the biscuit and mascarpone layers to form the body of the snowman. Place a marshmallow on top of the piped cream for the head.

- Using melted chocolate, stick an orange jelly bean on the marshmallow to make the nose of the snowman. Using a toothpick dipped in the melted chocolate, draw his face. You can also draw arms and buttons, if you like. Wrap a strawberry lace around the bottom of the marshmallow to make a scarf. Use your imagination and have fun!

- Serve immediately, or keep in the refrigerator until ready to serve.

Sun Bread with Pink Pralines

 Serves 8

 Preparation time
10 minutes
Cooking time
12–15 minutes

 Ingredients
2 sheets of ready-rolled puff pastry, chilled
50 g (2 oz) crushed pink pralines
1 egg yolk, beaten

 Specialist equipment
Small glass
Pastry brush

- Preheat the oven to 210°C (410°F/Gas Mark 7).

- On a baking sheet lined with baking parchment, unroll a sheet of ready-rolled puff pastry and sprinkle with the crushed pink pralines, leaving a 2 cm (¾ inch) border around the edge of the pastry.

- Unroll the remaining sheet of puff pastry and place it on top of the pastry sheet and pink pralines, pressing down well all around the edges to seal.

- Place a small glass or egg cup in the centre of the pastry and cut the pastry into 16 strips, radiating out from the glass and cutting to the edge of the pastry. Space the cuts evenly apart and press firmly to cut all the way through the pastry.

- Remove the glass and twist each strip into regular, even twists. If the pastry is too warm it will be difficult to work with: if necessary, place it in the freezer for 10 minutes.

- Take hold of 2 pieces of twisted pastry that are side-by-side and pinch the loose ends together to seal. Repeat with the remaining twisted pastry strips then brush the pastry with the beaten egg yolk to glaze.

- Bake in the preheated oven for 12–15 minutes, until golden brown. Remove from the oven and leave to cool for 5 minutes before transferring to a wire cooling rack to cool completely – or serve while still slightly warm if you prefer.

 *Yummy tip*

You can replace the puff pastry with brioche dough, if you prefer.

A golden sun to warm you up in winter …

My Fine Fir Tree

Makes 1

Preparation time
1 hour 20 minutes
Cooking time
20 minutes
Resting time
1 hour

Ingredients
Biscuits (cookies)
80 g (3 oz) butter, at room temperature
50 g (2 oz/¼ cup) caster (superfine) sugar
1 egg
190 g (6 ¾ oz/scant 1 ⅔ cup) plain (all-purpose) flour
Decoration
500 g (1 lb 2 oz) white fondant icing (sugar paste)
Edible glue
Silver sugar pearls or dragees
White sprinkles

Specialist equipment
Rolling pin
Set of star-shaped pastry cutters in at least 4 different sizes

- Using an electric whisk, beat the softened butter with the sugar until creamy. Add the egg and continue beating to combine. Add the flour, kneading quickly to incorporate, until you have a smooth, uniform dough. Shape the dough into a ball and leave in a cool place for 1 hour, wrapped in clingfilm (plastic wrap).

- Preheat the oven to 180°C (350°F/Gas Mark 4).

- Roll out the dough to a thickness of 5 mm (¼ inch) on a lightly floured worktop or between 2 sheets of baking parchment. Use the pastry cutters to cut out star shapes from the dough. Cut about 3 stars for each size of cutter.

- Arrange the biscuits on a baking sheet lined with baking parchment, leaving 1 cm (½ inch) between each biscuit to allow for them to spread. Bake in the preheated oven for 20 minutes then remove from the oven and leave to cool for 5 minutes before transferring to a wire cooling rack to cool completely.

- While the biscuits are baking, roll out the fondant icing to a thickness of 3 mm (¼ inch) on a worktop dusted with a little icing sugar. Use the pastry cutters to cut out the same number of icing stars as each size of biscuit.

- When the biscuits have cooled, place a few dots of edible glue on each one and lay over a fondant icing star to cover.

- Pile up the biscuits on a serving plate, starting with the larger ones on the base, progressing to the smallest at the top. Offset each biscuit to form a tapering fir-tree shape, with the points of each biscuit jutting out to form the branches. If you prefer, you can use the edible glue to stick the biscuits together to make it more stable.

- Use the edible glue to stick sugar pearls on the points of each star biscuit and finish with a dusting of white sprinkles.

Vanilla-Clementine Biscuit Cake

 Serves 4

Preparation time
30 minutes
Resting time
30 minutes
Cooking time
15 minutes

Ingredients
Biscuit (cookie) dough
500 g (1 lb 2 oz/4 cups) plain (all-purpose) flour
250 g (9 oz) butter, at room temperature
90 g (3 ¼ oz/generous cup) caster (superfine) sugar
70 g (2 ¼ oz/1 cup) ground almonds
pinch of salt
1 tbsp unsweetened cocoa powder
2 eggs
Mascarpone cream
150 g (5 oz) mascarpone
250 ml (8 ½ fl oz/1 cup) whipping cream
40 g (1 ½ oz/⅓ cup) icing (confectioners') sugar
Orange food colouring
Clementine/orange flavouring
Vanilla extract
Decoration
Mini gingerbread man biscuits (cookies)
Clementine segments
Sugar sprinkles

- Place all the biscuit ingredients, except the eggs, in the bowl of a stand mixer with a flat beater attached and mix together until the mixture has a grainy texture. Add the eggs and continue to mix until you have a smooth, uniform dough. Shape the dough into a ball then flatten it and leave in a cool place for 30 minutes, wrapped in clingfilm (plastic wrap).

- Preheat the oven to 160°C (320°F/Gas Mark 2).

- Divide the dough in half. Roll each dough half to a thickness of about 4 mm (¼ inch) on a lightly floured worktop or between 2 sheets of baking parchment. Using the pastry cutter, cut out a giant fir-tree shape from each half of the dough. Arrange each biscuit on a baking sheet lined with baking parchment. Bake in the preheated oven for 15 minutes then remove from the oven and leave to cool for 5 minutes before transferring to a wire cooling rack to cool completely.

- For the mascarpone cream, place the mascarpone, cream and icing sugar in the bowl of a stand mixer with a whisk attached and beat together until quite firm. Divide the cream equally between 2 bowls. Add a few drops of orange food colouring and clementine flavouring to one bowl and stir well to combine. Repeat with the vanilla extract.

- Fit 2 piping bags with star nozzles – fill one with the vanilla cream and the other with the clementine cream. Pipe alternate dots onto one of the biscuits. Place the second biscuit on top of the first and repeat the piping.

- Decorate with mini gingerbread men, clementine segments and sprinkles. Keep in a cool place until ready to serve.

 Specialist equipment
Stand mixer fitted with flat beater and whisk attachments
Giant fir-tree-shaped pastry cutter

2 x piping (pastry) bags
2 x 10–12 mm star nozzles (tips)

Orange Shortbread Crown

Makes 1

Preparation time
10 minutes
Cooking time
10–12 minutes
Resting time
30 minutes

Ingredients
130 g (4 oz) butter, melted
250 g (9 oz/2 cups) plain
(all-purpose) flour
2 ½ tsp baking powder
pinch of fleur de sel
100 g (3 ½ oz/scant ½ cup)
caster (superfine) sugar
1 egg plus 1 yolk
Grated zest of 1 orange

**For the royal icing (frosting)
ingredients see page 24**

Specialist equipment
Selection of star-shaped
pastry cutters in
different sizes

- Place all the shortbread ingredients together in a mixing bowl and mix carefully with a wooden spoon until you have a uniform dough. Shape the dough into a ball and leave in a cool place for 30 minutes, wrapped in clingfilm (plastic wrap).

- Preheat the oven to 180°C (350°F/Gas Mark 4).

- Roll out the dough to a thickness of 5 mm (¼ inch) on a lightly floured worktop or between 2 sheets of baking parchment. Cut out a large ring of dough, using a side plate as a template, and a glass or round pastry cutter to cut out the central hole. Use the star-shaped pastry cutters to cut out stars of dough in different sizes. Arrange the biscuits on a baking sheet lined with baking parchment, leaving 1 cm (½ inch) between each biscuit to allow for them to spread. Prick the surface of each shortbread evenly all over with a fork.

- Bake in the preheated oven for 10–12 minutes then remove from the oven and leave to cool for 5 minutes before transferring to a wire cooling rack to cool completely.

- For the royal icing method, see page 24. If you wish to use coloured icing, divide the mixture evenly into separate bowls for each colour. Add a few drops of food colouring to the icing and mix until you achieve the desired colour. Cover each bowl with clingfilm to prevent the icing from drying out when not in use.

- Decorate the star-shaped biscuits and place on the biscuit crown using a little icing to stick them on.

This crown can be made a few days in advance.

Merveilleux

 Makes 6

 Preparation time
30 minutes
Cooking time
45 minutes

Ingredients
Meringues
2 egg whites
pinch of salt
70 g (2 ½ oz/⅓ cup)
granulated sugar
70 g (2 ½ oz/generous
½ cup) icing (confectioners')
sugar plus extra for dusting
Chocolate mousse
200 g (7 oz) dark (bittersweet)
chocolate
400 ml (13 fl oz/generous
1 ½ cups) whipping cream,
chilled
Chocolate shavings
150 g (5 oz) bar dark
(bittersweet) chocolate

 Specialist equipment
Piping (pastry) bag
10 mm smooth nozzle (tip)
Bain-marie

- Preheat the oven to 120°C (250°F/Gas Mark ½).

- For the meringues, place the egg whites in a clean bowl, add the salt and beat using an electric whisk. Slowly add the granulated sugar as soon as the mixture starts to froth. Finally, add the icing sugar when the meringue starts to thicken and continue beating until stiff, glossy peaks form.

- Fit a piping bag with a smooth nozzle and fill the bag with the meringue, using a silicone spatula. Line a baking sheet with baking parchment and pipe 12 circles of meringue, each measuring 6–7 cm (2 ½ inches) in diameter. Dust each meringue with icing sugar.

- Bake in the preheated oven for 45 minutes then turn off the oven and leave the meringues inside to cool with the door left ajar. When the meringues are completely cool, remove from the oven and peel them from the baking parchment.

- For the mousse, finely chop the chocolate, place in a bowl and melt it in a bain-marie or microwave. Place the cream in a bowl and whip it, using an electric whisk, until it is slightly firm. Add the melted chocolate and keep whisking until the mixture is smooth, light and airy.

- For the chocolate shavings, use a peeler to grate chocolate into small flakes. Place in a shallow bowl and leave in a cool place until needed.

- When the meringues have cooled, assemble the merveilleux. Sandwich 2 meringues together with a generous layer of chocolate mousse. Spread the mousse over the surface of the meringues to form a dome. Finally coat the outside of the merveilleux with the chocolate shavings. Store in a cool place until ready to serve.

Gingerbread House

Makes 1

Preparation time
1 hour 45 minutes
Resting time
30 minutes
Cooking time
12 minutes

Ingredients
220 g (8 oz) butter
540 g (1 lb 3 oz/4 ⅓ cups) plain (all-purpose) flour
180 g (6 ½ oz/1 ¼ cups) wholemeal (wholewheat) flour
3 tbsp allspice
1 tsp bicarbonate of soda (baking soda) or baking powder
280 g (10 oz/1 ½ cups) muscovado sugar
2 eggs
160g (5 ½ oz/scant ½ cup) runny honey
For the royal icing (frosting) ingredients see page 24.
Decoration
Sweets (candies)
1 string of LED lights

Specialist equipment
Stand mixer fitted with flat beater attachment
1 or 2 disposable piping (pastry) bags

- Place the butter with 360 g (12 oz) plain flour into the stand mixer and beat together until the mix has a grainy texture. Add the remaining dry ingredients and mix well to fully combine. Add one egg at a time, then the honey, mixing continuously as you do so, until you have a uniform dough. Shape the dough into a ball and leave in a cool place for 30 minutes, wrapped in clingfilm (plastic wrap).

- Preheat the oven to 180°C (350°F/Gas Mark 4).

- Roll out the dough to a thickness of 5 mm (¼ inch) on a lightly floured worktop or between 2 sheets of baking parchment. Cut out the 4 sides of the house (2 ends with the roof apex, a window and a door; 2 lower walls with windows) and the 2 sides of the roof, or use gingerbread house pastry cutters if you have them. Cut around a plate to make a large round base for the house to rest on. Use any leftover dough to make fir trees or snowmen for decoration. Arrange the biscuits on a baking sheet lined with baking parchment, leaving 1 cm (½ inch) between each to allow for them to spread. Bake for 12 minutes then remove and leave to cool for 5 minutes before transferring to a wire cooling rack to cool completely.

- For the royal icing method, see page 24.

- To assemble the house, cut off a little more from the tip of the piping bag and pipe a generous line of icing along every edge of each wall. Assemble all 4 walls of the house, passing a string of LED lights through one of the wall joints, taking care to ensure the on/off button is on the outside. Gently hold the roof in place for a few seconds until it is secure. Hide the join along the ridge of the roof and at the gable ends by piping icing along them to look like icicles. Finish by sticking some sweets on the house and a few fir-tree or snowman biscuits in the garden.

- To decorate the house, fill a disposable piping bag with the icing and cut off the tip to 1 or 2 mm. Pipe the details on the house: roof tiles, window and door frames, and any other patterns you like.

Ice Cream Crown with Chestnuts

Serves 6

Preparation time
50 minutes
Freezing time
12 hours

Ingredients
Vanilla ice cream
1 vanilla pod (bean)
550 ml (18 ½ fl oz/2 ⅓ cups)
whole (full-fat) milk
150 ml (5 fl oz/scant ⅔ cup)
single (light) cream
3 egg yolks
100 g (3 ½ oz/scant ½ cup)
caster (superfine) sugar
16 mini meringues
**Chestnut vermicelli
decoration**
500 g (1 lb 2 oz) chestnut
purée (unsweetened)
500 g (1 1lb 2oz) chestnut
cream or spread
100 ml (3 ½ fl oz/scant
½ cup) double (heavy) cream
Meringue kisses, to decorate

Specialist equipment
Sugar thermometer
Ice cream maker
Large silicone savarin or
ring mould
Silicone spatula
Stand mixer fitted with a flat
beater attachment
Piping (pastry) bag
Vermicelli nozzle (tip)

- Using a knife, split the vanilla pod and scrape out the seeds. Pour the milk and 150 ml (5 fl oz/scant ⅔ cups) single cream into a saucepan, add the vanilla pod and seeds and bring to a boil. As soon as it starts to boil, remove from the heat and set aside.

- Using an electric whisk, beat the egg yolks with the sugar until the mixture turns pale. Remove the vanilla pod from the hot milk and pour half the milk into the yolk mix, stirring to combine. Repeat with the remaining hot milk, stirring continuously as you do so.

- Return the mix to the saucepan and heat, stirring, until it reaches 84°C (184°F) on a sugar thermometer, or the mixture coats the back of a spoon. Set aside to cool, then pour into an ice cream maker and churn for 40 minutes.

- Fill three quarters of a silicone savarin or ring mould with the ice cream. Arrange the meringues evenly around the mould then pour over the remaining ice cream and use a silicone spatula to level off the top. Place in the freezer for 12 hours.

- Before serving, decorate the crown. Place the chestnut purée, chestnut cream and 100 ml (3 ½ fl oz/scant ½ cup) double cream in the bowl of a stand mixer with a flat beater attached. Beat together until smooth and firm but still malleable.

- Remove the ice cream from the mould. Fit a piping bag with a vermicelli nozzle and pipe the chestnut topping over the ice cream crown in a side-to-side motion, working from the inside of the ring to the outside and back again. Finish off with meringues and pieces of chestnut, if you'd like.

- Cut into slices and serve immediately.

Yummy tip

Use homemade ice cream: shop-bought ice cream
may be too soft.

Triple-chocolate Log

 Serves 6

Preparation time
40 minutes
Cooking time
12–15 minutes
Freezing time
4 hours

Ingredients
Sponge
2 eggs
60 g (2 oz/generous ¼ cup)
caster (superfine) sugar
60 g (2 oz/½ cup) self-raising
(self-rising) flour
Soaking syrup
50 g (2 oz/scant ¼ cup) caster
(superfine) sugar
50 ml (1 ¾ fl oz/3 tbsp) water
50 ml (1 ¾ fl oz/3 tbsp) rum
Chocolate mousses
450 ml (15 fl oz/1 ¾ cups)
whipping cream
150 g (5 oz) white chocolate
150 g (5 oz) milk chocolate
150 g (5 oz) dark (bittersweet)
chocolate
Glaze
6 sheets of gelatine
250 ml (8 ½ fl oz/1 cup) single
(light) cream
250 g (9 oz/generous 1 cup)
caster (superfine) sugar

 Specialist equipment
Bain-marie
Log cake tin (pan)
Sugar thermometer

- Preheat the oven to 180°C (350°F/Gas Mark 4).

- Beat the eggs and sugar in a mixing bowl until the mixture doubles in volume. Gently fold in the flour until fully incorporated. Line a baking tray with baking parchment and spread the dough out on the paper to the same length and width as the log cake tin. Bake for 12–15 minutes, then remove and leave to cool.

- For the syrup, bring the sugar and water to a boil, then remove from the heat and stir in the rum. Set aside to cool.

- For the mousses, whip the cream until quite firm. Divide the whipped cream equally into 3 bowls. Finely chop the white chocolate and melt it in a bain-marie or microwave. When it is fully melted remove it from the heat. Repeat with the milk and dark chocolates, and set aside in separate bowls.

- Add the melted white chocolate to one of the bowls of whipped cream and whisk to combine. Repeat with the other chocolates and cream. Place a layer of mousse in the log cake tin, and repeat with the remaining mousses.

- Brush the syrup over the sponge to moisten it, then place it on top of the mousses in the log cake tin, trimming the edges to fit as necessary. Freeze for a minimum of 4 hours, ideally overnight.

- When you are ready to serve, prepare the glaze. Soak the sheets of gelatine in cold water for 5 minutes to soften. Heat the single cream in a saucepan. In another saucepan, boil the sugar with a dash of water to make a caramel. When the caramel is well coloured, pour in the warm cream, stirring continuously. Remove the gelatine sheets from the bowl and squeeze out any excess water, then add to the caramel mixture. Stir until completely dissolved and leave to cool until it reaches 27°C (80°F) on a sugar thermometer.

- Remove the chocolate log from the cake tin and place it on a wire cooling rack over a tray. Cover the whole log with the glaze, allowing any excess to drip onto the plate. Transfer to a serving plate and add extra decoration, if you like, before serving.

Lemon and Raspberry Log

Serves 6

Preparation time
50 minutes
Cooking time
15 minutes
Freezing time
6 hours

Ingredients
Pistachio dacquoises
25 g (1 oz/¼ cup) ground almonds
80 g (3 oz/¾ cup) ground pistachios
45 g (1 ¾ oz/scant ¼ cup) caster (superfine) sugar
105 g (3½ oz/generous ¾ cup) icing (confectioners') sugar
4 egg whites
Raspberry mousse
3 sheets of gelatine
250 ml (8 ½ fl oz/1 cup) raspberry coulis
250 ml (8 ½ fl oz/1 cup) whipping cream, chilled
Lemon mousse
3 sheets of gelatine
200 ml (7 fl oz/scant 1 cup) lemon juice
60 g (2 oz/generous ¼ cup) caster (superfine) sugar
250 ml (8 ½ fl oz/1 cup) whipping cream
Glaze
150 ml (5 fl oz/scant ⅔ cup) neutral mirror glaze
Red and gold food colouring
Pistachio nibs

- Preheat the oven to 180°C (350°F/Gas Mark 4). For the pistachio dacquoises, mix the ground nuts and sugars together in a mixing bowl. Place the egg whites in a clean bowl and beat until stiff peaks form. Fold in the nuts and sugars. Line a baking tray with baking parchment and spread half the dacquoise mix out on the paper to the same length and width as the log cake tin. Repeat with the other half of the mix. Bake for 10 minutes, then remove from the oven and leave to cool.

- For the raspberry mousse, soak the sheets of gelatine in cold water for 5 minutes to soften. Heat one-third of the raspberry coulis in a saucepan. Remove the gelatine sheets from the bowl and squeeze out any excess water, then add to the hot coulis and stir until completely dissolved. Add the reserved coulis. Whip the cream until quite firm then fold into the raspberry coulis mix, using a silicone spatula.

- For the lemon mousse, soak the sheets of gelatine in cold water for 5 minutes to soften. Sweeten the lemon juice by mixing in the sugar. Heat one-third of the lemon juice in a saucepan. Remove the gelatine sheets from the bowl and squeeze out any excess water, then add to the hot lemon juice and stir until completely dissolved. Add the reserved lemon juice. Whip the cream until quite firm, then fold into the lemon mix. Spoon the lemon mousse into the tin and place a pistachio dacquoise biscuit on top, then add the raspberry mousse and smooth with the back of a spoon. Add the second dacquoise biscuit on top and place the log tin in the freezer for 6 hours.

- Remove the log from the cake tin and leave in a cool place to defrost for 4 hours. When you are ready to serve, prepare the glaze. Gently warm the neutral mirror glaze and add a few drops of food colouring to colour it. Place the log on a wire rack over a tray and pour over the glaze to cover the whole log, allowing any excess to drip onto the plate. Press the pistachio nibs into the glaze, along the sides of the log to decorate, before serving.

Specialist equipment
Log cake tin
Baking tray (pan)

Vanilla and Caramel Log

Serves 6

Preparation time
50 minutes
Cooking time
12–15 minutes
Refrigeration time
48 hours + 4 hours freezing

Ingredients
Whipped vanilla ganache
1 ½ sheets of gelatine
400 ml (13 fl oz/generous
1 ½ cups) whipping cream
1 vanilla pod (bean)
95 g (3 ½ oz) bar white
chocolate
Caramel filling
1 ½ sheets of gelatine
200 ml (7 fl oz/scant 1 cup)
single (light) cream
100 g (3 ½ oz/scant ½ cup)
caster (superfine) sugar
15 g (½ oz) glucose (corn)
syrup (or honey)
2 eggs plus 1 yolk
Sponge
2 eggs
60 g (2 oz/generous ¼ cup)
caster (superfine) sugar
60 g (2 oz/½ cup) self-raising
(self-rising) flour
White velvet spray (to decorate)
Soaking syrup
70 g (2 ¼ oz/scant ⅓ cup)
caster (superfine) sugar
70 ml (2 ½ fl oz/5 tbsp) water
2 tbsp vanilla extract

Specialist Equipment
See page 72

- Prepare the ganache 2 days in advance. Soak the sheets of gelatine in cold water for 5 minutes to soften. Pour the cream into a saucepan and add the scraped vanilla seeds and pod. Gently heat until just boiling then remove from the heat and leave to infuse for 15 minutes. Chop the white chocolate and melt it in a bain-marie or microwave. Remove the vanilla pod from the milk then slowly pour it into the chocolate, stirring until fully incorporated. Remove the gelatine sheets from the bowl and squeeze out any excess water, then add to the chocolate mix and stir until completely dissolved. Cover the bowl with clingfilm (plastic wrap) and leave in the refrigerator for 48 hours.

- Prepare the caramel filling one day in advance. Soak the gelatine in cold water. Heat the single cream in a saucepan and keep it warm. In another saucepan, boil the sugar, 25 ml (5 tsp) water and the glucose syrup to make a caramel. When the caramel is well coloured, pour in the warm cream, stirring continuously. Beat the eggs and pour into a saucepan, off the heat. Pour in the caramel, whisking continuously. Heat to 82°C (180°F), stirring continuously. Drain the gelatine sheets as above, then add to the caramel mixture and stir until completely dissolved. Pour the mixture into the hollow insert from a cake tin (pan) and place in the freezer overnight.

- To make the sponge, preheat the oven to 180°C (350°F/Gas Mark 4). Beat the eggs with the sugar until the mixture doubles in volume. Gently fold in the flour until fully incorporated. Line a baking tray with baking parchment and spread the dough out on the paper. Bake for 12–15 minutes, then remove from the oven and leave to cool. For the syrup, place the sugar and water in a saucepan and bring to a boil. Remove from the heat and add the vanilla extract. Allow to cool.

- To assemble the log, whisk the vanilla ganache until quite firm. Spoon the ganache into the log cake tin until half filled. Remove the caramel filling from the cake tin insert and place it on the middle of the ganache. Spoon the remaining ganache over the top and smooth with the back of a spoon. Brush the syrup over the sponge to moisten it, then place it on top of the ganache in the log cake tin, trimming the edges to fit. Freeze for a minimum of 4 hours.

- To serve, remove the log from the tin, spray with the white velvet spray and defrost in a cool place for 4 hours.

Chocolate and Raspberry Log

Serves 6

Preparation time
50 minutes
Cooking time
12–15 minutes
Refrigeration time
Overnight + 4 hours

Ingredients
Whipped vanilla ganache
1 ½ sheets of gelatine
400 ml (13 fl oz/generous
1 ½ cups) whipping cream
1 vanilla pod (bean)
95 g (3 ½ oz) white chocolate
Chocolate sponge
4 eggs
80 g (3 oz/⅓ cup) caster
(superfine) sugar
30 g (1 oz/¼ cup)
unsweetened cocoa powder
120 g (4 oz/scant 1 cup)
self-raising (self-rising) flour
1 tsp baking powder
100 g (3 ½ oz/generous
¾ cup) raspberries
Icing (confectioners') sugar,
for dusting
Soaking syrup
70 g (2 ½ oz/scant ⅓ cup)
caster (superfine) sugar
70 ml (2 ½ fl oz/5 tbsp) water
2 tbsp vanilla extract

Specialist equipment
Bain-marie
Swiss roll baking tin (pan)

- Prepare the ganache one day in advance. Soak the sheets of gelatine in cold water for 5 minutes to soften. Pour the cream into a saucepan, remove the seeds from the vanilla pod and add to the milk, along with the split pod. Gently heat until just boiling then remove from the heat and leave to infuse for 15 minutes. Finely chop the white chocolate and melt it in a bain-marie or microwave. Remove the vanilla pod from the warm milk then slowly pour it into the melted chocolate, stirring continuously until fully incorporated. Remove the gelatine sheets from the bowl and squeeze out any excess water, then add to the hot chocolate mix and stir until completely dissolved. Cover the bowl with clingfilm (plastic wrap) and leave in the refrigerator overnight.

- Preheat the oven to 180°C (350°F/Gas Mark 4).

- To make the chocolate sponge, beat the eggs with the caster sugar in a mixing bowl until the mixture doubles in volume. Add the cocoa powder, flour and baking powder, and mix until fully incorporated.

- Grease a swiss roll tin and pour in the sponge batter, spreading it out evenly. Bake for 12–15 minutes, then remove from the oven and leave to cool slightly before rolling.

- While the sponge is cooking, whisk the vanilla ganache until it is quite firm. Spread the ganache over the sponge, when it is still slightly warm, in a perfectly even layer. Arrange the raspberries evenly, reserving some for decoration. Roll the sponge from the shorter edge, pressing firmly as you roll. Leave to cool completely.

- For the syrup, place the sugar and water in a saucepan and bring to a boil. Remove from the heat and add the vanilla extract. Once cool, brush the log with the syrup to moisten it, then wrap it in clingfilm and leave in the refrigerator to cool for at least 4 hours.

- Place on a serving plate, dust with icing sugar and decorate with a few raspberries.

Praline and Lemon Log

Serves 6

Preparation time
50 minutes
Cooking time
12–15 minutes
Refrigeration time
4 hours

Ingredients
5 eggs
155 g (5 oz/generous
⅔ cup) caster
(superfine) sugar
1 tbsp praline paste
1 tsp baking powder
170 g (6 oz/generous
1 ⅓ cups) plain (all-purpose)
flour
200 g (7 oz/⅔ cup) lemon
curd
Hazelnut (filbert) nibs

Specialist equipment
Swiss roll baking tin (pan)

- Preheat the oven to 180°C (350°F/Gas Mark 4).

- Using an electric whisk, beat together the eggs, sugar and praline paste in a mixing bowl. Whisk until the mixture doubles in volume, then gently fold in the baking powder and flour.

- Grease a swiss roll baking tin and pour in the sponge batter, spreading it out evenly. Bake in the preheated oven for 12–15 minutes. Remove from the oven and leave to cool slightly before rolling.

- Spread the lemon curd over the sponge when it is still slightly warm, in an even layer. Roll the sponge, from the shorter edge, pressing firmly as you roll. Leave to cool completely.

- Wrap the log tightly in clingfilm (plastic wrap) and leave in the refrigerator to cool for at least 4 hours.

- Place the log on a serving plate and decorate with hazelnut nibs.

When lemon meets praline ...

Yummy tip

Decorate with a few meringue kisses, if you like.

Raspberry and Blueberry Log

 Serves 6

 Preparation time
50 minutes
Cooking time
12–15 minutes
Freezing time
4 hours + overnight

Ingredients
Blueberry mousse
3 sheets of gelatine
250 ml (8 ½ fl oz/1 cup)
blueberry coulis
250 ml (8 ½ fl oz/1 cup)
whipping cream, chilled
Lemon sponge cake
2 eggs
60 g (2 oz/generous ¼ cup)
caster (superfine) sugar
Grated zest of 1 lemon
1 tsp baking powder
60 g (2 oz/½ cup) self-raising
(self-rising) flour
Pink velvet spray, to decorate
Raspberry filling
3 sheets of gelatine
250 ml (8 ½ fl oz/1 cup)
raspberry coulis
250 ml (8 ½ fl oz/1 cup)
whipping cream

 Specialist equipment
Cake tin (pan) with insert,
only the insert is required
Log cake tin (pan)

- Make the log the day before you wish to serve it.

- For the blueberry mousse, soak the sheets of gelatine in cold water for 5 minutes to soften. Heat one-third of the blueberry coulis in a saucepan. Remove the gelatine sheets from the bowl and squeeze out any excess water, then add to the hot coulis and stir until completely dissolved. Add the reserved coulis. Whip the cream until quite firm, then fold it into the blueberry coulis mix using a silicone spatula. Pour the mixture into the insert from a cake tin and place in the freezer for a minimum of 4 hours.

- Preheat the oven to 180°C (350°F/Gas Mark 4).

- To make the lemon sponge, beat the eggs with the sugar in a mixing bowl until the mixture doubles in volume. Gently mix in the lemon zest, baking powder and flour. Line a baking tray with baking parchment and spread the mix on the paper in an even rectangle. Bake for 12–15 minutes, then remove from the oven and leave to cool in the tray. Cut out a rectangle measuring 30 cm x 8 cm (12 inches x 3 inches). Cover with clingfilm (plastic wrap) and set aside.

- When the blueberry mousse has frozen, make the raspberry mousse using the same method. Spoon the raspberry mousse into the log tin until it is half filled. Remove the frozen blueberry mousse from the cake tin insert and place it on top of the raspberry mousse so that it lays along the centre of the log. Spoon the remaining raspberry mousse over the top and smooth with the back of a spoon. Place the lemon sponge on top and place in the freezer overnight.

- When ready to serve, remove the log from the tin, spray with the pink velvet spray, place on a serving plate and leave to defrost in a cool place for 4 hours before serving.

Mango and Coconut Log

 Serves 6

Preparation time
50 minutes
Cooking time
10 minutes
Freezing time
3 hours + 6 hours

Ingredients
Coconut mousse
2 ½ sheets of gelatine
175 ml (6 fl oz/¾ cup) coconut milk
60 g (2 oz/generous ¼ cup) white caster (superfine) sugar
40 g (1 ½ oz/scant ½ cup) desiccated coconut
175 ml (6 fl oz/¾ cup) whipping cream, chilled
Dacquoise
85 g (3 oz/scant cup) desiccated coconut
100 g (3 ½ oz/generous ¾ cup) icing (confectioners') sugar
35 g (1 ¼ oz/3 tbsp) caster (superfine) sugar
3 egg whites
Mango mousse
4 ½ sheets of gelatine
50 g (2 oz) tinned mangoes
300 ml (10 fl oz/1 ¼ cups) whipping cream
Topping
150 g (5 oz) white chocolate
105 ml (3 ½ fl oz/scant ½ cup) single (light) cream
150 g (5 oz/2 ½ cups) grated (shredded) coconut

- For the coconut mousse, soak the sheets of gelatine in cold water for 5 minutes to soften. Heat the coconut milk in a sauce-pan with the sugar, stirring until the sugar dissolves. Remove the gelatine sheets from the bowl and squeeze out any excess water, add to the hot coconut milk along with the desiccated coconut and stir until completely dissolved. Allow to cool.

- Whip the cream until quite firm. Fold the cream into the coconut mix using a silicone spatula, then pour into the cake tin insert and place in the freezer for a minimum of 3 hours.

- Preheat the oven to 180°C (350°F/Gas Mark 4). For the dacquoise, mix the coconut and sugars together in a mixing bowl. Place the egg whites in a clean bowl and beat until stiff peaks form. Fold in the coconut and sugars. Line a baking tray with baking parchment and spread the dacquoise mix out along the tin. Bake for 10 minutes, then remove and leave to cool.

- For the mango mousse, soak the sheets of gelatine (as above). Purée the mangoes in a blender, then heat one-third of the purée in a saucepan. Add the drained gelatine sheets to the hot purée and stir until dissolved. Add the reserved purée.

- Whip the cream until quite firm, then fold it into the purée mix using a silicone spatula. Spoon the mango mousse into the tin until it is half filled. Remove the frozen coconut filling from the insert and place it on the middle of the mango mousse. Spoon the remaining mango mousse over the top and smooth the surface with the back of a spoon. Place the dacquoise biscuit on top of the mousse and place the tin in the freezer for 6 hours.

- Remove the log from the cake tin and leave to defrost for 4 hours. When you are ready to serve, prepare the topping. Chop the white chocolate and melt in a bain-marie or microwave with the single cream. Place the log on a wire cooling rack over a tray and pour the topping over the whole log. Immediately sprinkle the grated coconut over so it sticks to the topping. Serve.

 Specialist equipment
Insert only of a cake tin (pan)   Log cake tin (pan)
Blender or food processor   Bain-marie

Candy Cane with Aniseed

 Serves 6

Preparation time
50 minutes
Cooking time
12–15 minutes
Refrigeration time
48 hours + 4 hours (freezing)
+ 6 hours (freezing)

Ingredients
Whipped aniseed ganache
1 ½ sheets of gelatine
95 g (3 ½ oz) white chocolate
400 ml (13 fl oz/generous
1 ½ cups) whipping cream
1 tsp anise seeds
Raspberry mousse
3 sheets of gelatine
250 ml (8 ½ fl oz/1 cup)
raspberry coulis
250 ml (8 ½ fl oz/1 cup)
whipping cream, chilled
Topping
200g (7 oz) white chocolate
Red food colouring
White velvet spray
Aniseed sponge
4 eggs
110 g (3 ¾ oz/scant ½ cup)
caster (superfine) sugar
½ tsp ground aniseed
1 tsp baking powder
120 g (4 oz/scant 1 cup) self-
raising (self-rising) flour

 Specialist equipment
Bain-marie
Insert only of a cake tin (pan)
Large silicone candy cane
cake mould

- Prepare the aniseed ganache 2 days in advance. Soak the sheets of gelatine in cold water for 5 minutes to soften. Chop the chocolate and melt it in a bain-marie or microwave. Pour the cream into a saucepan with the anise seeds. Gently heat until just boiling then remove from the heat to infuse for 15 minutes. Pour into the melted chocolate, stirring to combine. Remove the gelatine sheets from the bowl and squeeze out any excess water, then add to the chocolate aniseed mix and stir well until completely dissolved. Cover the bowl with clingfilm (plastic wrap) and leave in the refrigerator for 48 hours.

- For the raspberry mousse, soak the sheets of gelatine (as above). Heat one-third of the coulis in a saucepan. Add the drained gelatine sheets to the hot coulis and stir until dissolved. Add the reserved coulis. Whip the cream until quite firm, then fold it into the coulis mix using a silicone spatula. Pour the mixture into the cake tin insert and place in the freezer for 4 hours.

- Chop the white chocolate and melt it in a bain-marie or microwave. Add a few drops of the food colouring and mix until it's a deep red colour. Using a brush, fill the recesses of the mould with the coloured chocolate to form the stripes of the candy cane. Place in the freezer.

- Make the sponge one day in advance. Preheat the oven to 180°C (350°F/Gas Mark 4). Beat the eggs with the sugar until doubled in volume. Fold in the aniseed, baking powder and flour. Line a baking tray with baking parchment and spread the sponge mix in, using the mould as a template. Bake for 12–15 minutes, then remove from the oven and allow to cool in the tray.

- To assemble the log, whisk the aniseed ganache until quite firm. Spoon the ganache into the mould until it is half filled. Place the frozen raspberry mousse on top of the ganache. Spoon the remaining ganache over the top and smooth with the back of a spoon. Place the sponge on top of the ganache in the mould, trimming the edges to fit as necessary. Freeze for 6 hours.

- Remove the cane from the mould. Protect the chocolate stripes with strips of baking parchment and spray any exposed parts with the white velvet. Defrost slowly for 6 hours before serving.

Pistachio Crown

Serves 8

Preparation time
20 minutes
Cooking time
35 minutes

Ingredients
175 g (6 oz) butter
120 g (4 oz/scant 1 cup)
self-raising (self-rising) flour
175 g (6 oz/generous
1 ⅔ cups) ground almonds
2 tbsp pistachio paste
Green food colouring
(optional)
6 egg whites
100 g (3 ½ oz/generous
¾ cup) raspberries
Decoration
150 g (5 oz) white chocolate
70 ml (2 ½ fl oz/5 tbsp) single
(light) cream
100 g (3 ½ oz/⅔ cup) shelled
unsalted green pistachios
Raspberries

Specialist equipment
Muslin (cheesecloth)
Silicone crown or ring
mould

- Preheat the oven to 180°C (350°F°/Gas Mark 4).

- Melt the butter in a saucepan and let it bubble until it has a nutty smell. Filter it through muslin (cheesecloth) and set aside.

- Place the egg whites in a clean bowl and beat with an electric whisk until stiff peaks form. Mix the flour and ground almonds together in a mixing bowl, then add the pistachio paste, melted butter and a touch of food colouring, if using. Mix until you have a uniform batter then gently fold into the whisked egg whites.

- Pour one-third of the sponge batter into the crown mould. Distribute the raspberries evenly over the batter then pour the remaining batter on top. Bake in the preheated oven for 35 minutes. Remove from the oven and set aside to cool in the tin for 10 minutes before transferring to a wire cooling rack to cool completely.

- Finely chop the white chocolate, place in a bowl with the single cream and melt in a bain-marie or microwave. Roughly chop the pistachios.

- Place a tray under the cooling rack and pour the melted chocolate and cream mixture over the crown to completely cover it, allowing any excess topping to drip onto the tray. Immediately sprinkle the chopped pistachios over, so they stick to the topping. Finish by decorating with fresh raspberries or any decoration of your choice.

Be the king or queen of Christmas!

Yummy tip

You can replace the raspberries with baked apples or the zest of an orange.

Gingerbread

Serves 8

Preparation time
10 minutes
Cooking time
1 hour 15 minutes
Resting time
24 hours

Ingredients
250 g (9 oz/2 cups) plain (all-purpose) flour
100 g (3 ½ oz/generous ½ cup) muscovado sugar
2 tsp allspice
1 tsp ground cinnamon
1 tsp green aniseed powder
1 tsp ground ginger (optional)
250g (9 oz/¾ cup) honey
2 ½ tsp baking powder or 2 tsp bicarbonate of soda (baking soda)
11 g (1 ½ sachets/1 tbsp) vanilla sugar
100 ml (3 ½ fl oz/scant ½ cup) whole (full-fat) milk
2 eggs
Apricot or orange jam (jelly), to glaze
Icing (confectioners') sugar, for dusting
Cinnamon sticks, star anise or candied orange, to decorate (optional)

Specialist equipment
Loaf tin (pan), greased or lined with baking parchment

- Preheat the oven to 160°C (320°F/Gas Mark 2).

- Mix the flour, muscavado sugar and all the spices together in a mixing bowl and set aside. Place the honey in a saucepan and gently heat until just boiling. Pour into the dry ingredients, add the baking powder or the bicarbonate of soda, vanilla sugar and milk, and stir until you have a uniform mixture. Add the eggs and mix until fully incorporated.

- Pour the batter into a greased or lined loaf tin and bake in the preheated oven for about 1 hour 15 minutes. Do not open the oven door until at least 45 minutes of cooking time have lapsed or the loaf may sink in the middle. The loaf is done when a skewer inserted in the centre comes out clean and dry. Remove from the oven and set aside to cool in the tin for 10 minutes before transferring to a wire cooling rack to cool completely.

- When the gingerbread has cooled, remove it from the tin and wrap well in clingfilm (plastic wrap). Cover with a clean tea (dish) towel and leave for 24 hours for the rich flavour to develop.

- When ready to serve, dissolve a tablespoon of apricot or orange jam with a little hot water and brush over the top of the loaf to glaze. Dust the top with icing sugar and decorate with cinnamon sticks, star anise or candied orange, if you like.

Stollen

 Serves 10

 Preparation time
40 minutes
Cooking time
35 minutes
Resting time
1 hour 30 minutes

Ingredients
170 g (6 oz/1 ⅓ cups) mixed dried fruits of your preference
180 g (6 ¼ oz) white marzipan (sugared almond paste)
1 egg plus 1 yolk
7 g (1 sachet/2 ¼ tsp) fast action (active dry) yeast or 20g (¾ oz/1 ⅓ tbsp) fresh baker's yeast
150 ml (5 fl oz/scant ⅔ cup) whole (full-fat) milk, warmed
250 g (9 oz/2 cups) plain (all-purpose) flour
40 g (1 ½ oz) butter, at room temperature
30 g (1 oz/2 ⅓ tbsp) caster (superfine) sugar
Grated zest of 1 orange or 1 lemon
Icing (confectioners') sugar, for dusting

Specialist equipment
Stand mixer with dough hook attachment

- Soak the dried fruits in warm water for 15 minutes. Drain and set aside.

- Knead the egg yolk into the marzipan until fully incorporated then roll it into a long, 30 x 3 cm (12 x 1 inch) cylinder and set aside.

- Place the yeast in the bowl of a stand mixer, pour in the warm milk and add half the flour. Leave to stand for 30 minutes to activate the yeast.

- Add the remaining flour, the butter, whole egg and caster sugar and knead, in the stand mixer, for a minimum of 10 minutes. When the dough is soft and not too sticky, add the dried fruits and the citrus zest and continue kneading until you have a uniform, elastic dough. Cover with a clean tea (dish) towel and leave to stand until it doubles in volume.

- Using a rolling pin coated with flour, roll out the dough into an oval, about 2.5 cm (1 inch) thick. Place the roll of marzipan along the middle of the dough. Fold one-third of the dough over the marzipan from the long side of the oval to just cover the marzipan (do not fold it all the way over to the opposite edge of the dough), repeat with the other side, pressing the top and bottom ends down well to enclose the marzipan. Leave to stand for at least 1 hour in a well-ventilated place.

- Preheat the oven to 190°C (375°F/Gas Mark 5).

- Place the stollen on a baking sheet lined with baking parchment and bake in the preheated oven for 35 minutes: if the dough colours too much, lower the oven temperature to 160°C (320°F/Gas Mark 2).

- Remove from the oven and set aside to cool for 10 minutes before transferring to a wire cooling rack to cool completely.

- When the stollen is cool dust the top with a generous layer of icing sugar. Cut into slices and serve.

Sugared Pretzels

 Serves 8

 Preparation time
30 minutes
Cooking time
20 minutes
Resting time
3 hours

Ingredients
500 g (1 lb 2 oz/4 cups) plain (all-purpose) flour
pinch of salt
20 g (¾ oz/1 ⅓ tbsp) fresh baker's yeast
5 eggs plus 1 yolk, at room temperature
200 g (7 oz) butter, at room temperature
1 tbsp orange blossom water
50 g (2 oz/¼ cup) caster (superfine) sugar
100 g (3 ½ oz/ ½ cup) pearl sugar

Specialist equipment
Stand mixer with dough hook attachment

- Place the flour, salt and yeast in the bowl of a stand mixer fitted with a dough attachment. Switch the mixer on at high speed then add the whole eggs, mixing continuously as you do so. Reduce the speed to medium and mix for 8 minutes.

- Cut the softened butter into small pieces and add to the mix with the orange blossom water and caster sugar. Knead for 10 minutes until the dough comes away from the sides of the bowl.

- Cover the bowl with a clean tea (dish) towel and leave to rise for 1 hour at room temperature.

- Knock back the dough to its original volume by hitting it with a spatula or a knife but without kneading it. Set aside in a cool place for 1 hour 30 minutes.

- Preheat the oven to 180°C (350°F/Gas Mark 4).

- Divide the dough into 16 balls of equal size. Using the palm of your hand, roll each ball of dough into a long thin tube. Curl and twist each tube into a pretzel and place on a baking sheet covered in baking parchment. Leave to prove for 30 minutes.

- Beat the egg yolk and brush over the pretzels using a pastry brush. Sprinkle generously with pearl sugar and bake in the preheated oven for 20 minutes until golden brown. Serve hot or warm

You can freeze the pretzels immediately after shaping them. Defrost as you need them, then glaze with egg yolk, sprinkle with pearl sugar and bake in the oven as normal.

Panettone with Candied Fruits

 Serves 8

 Preparation time
3 hours
Cooking time
1 hour
Resting time
3 nights + 6 hours + 24 hours

Ingredients
Leaven
50 g (2 oz/⅓ cup) oat flour
5 g (¼ oz/2 tsp) malt flour
60 ml (2 fl oz/¼ cup) whole (full-fat) milk
30 g (1 oz/2 tbsp) fresh baker's yeast
Dough
350 g (12 oz/3 cups) oat flour
2 eggs
130 g (4 oz/scant ⅔ cup) caster (superfine) sugar
50 ml (1 ¾ fl oz/3 tbsp) whole (full-fat) milk
1 tsp honey
100 g (3 ½ oz) butter + 1 tbsp + 1 knob, at room temperature
Grated zest of 1 orange
Grated zest of ½ a lemon
75 g (2 ½ oz/scant ⅔ cup) candied fruits
75 g (2 ½ oz/scant ⅔ cup) raisins or 180 g (6 ¼ oz/1 cup) chocolate chips

 Specialist equipment
Stand mixer with dough hook attachment
Paper panettone mould
2 wooden skewers

- Prepare the leaven 2 days in advance: mix all the ingredients together in a mixing bowl until smooth with a consistent texture. Cover the bowl with clingfilm (plastic wrap) and leave to rest overnight at room temperature.

- The next day, place 200 g (7 oz/1 ¼ cups) oat flour, the leaven, 1 egg, 65 g (2 ¼ oz/¼ cup) sugar, the milk and honey into a stand mixer fitted with a dough attachment. Knead for 20 minutes. When the dough starts to come away from the sides of the bowl, gradually add 40 g (1 ½ oz) of softened butter and knead for another 7–8 minutes. Wrap the dough in clingfilm and leave to rest overnight in a cool place.

- Let the dough rest for 8 hours at room temperature the night before baking. Return the dough to the mixer and add the remaining egg, sugar, flour and citrus zests. Knead for 20 minutes. Gradually add the remaining butter, candied fruits and raisins or chocolate chips.

- Shape the dough into a ball and place in a paper panettone mould. Brush the top of the dough with melted butter to stop it from forming a crust and leave to rise for 6 hours at room temperature. Score a cross on the top of the panettone and place a knob of butter in the middle.

- Preheat the oven to 200°C (400°F/Gas Mark 6), place the panettone in the oven then lower the temperature to 180°C (350°F/Gas Mark 4).

- Bake for 20 minutes, then cover with foil. After a further 20 minutes, lower to 150°C (300°F/Gas Mark 1). The panettone is done when a wooden skewer inserted in the centre comes out clean and dry.

- Remove the panettone from the oven and insert 2 wooden skewers at right angles to each other, near the base. Turn the panettone upside down and use the skewers to suspend it over a large saucepan, making sure it doesn't touch the bottom or sides of the pan. This will help the panettone to dry a little. Leave for 24 hours before eating.

Christmas Brioche

Makes 2/Serves 8

Preparation time
30 minutes
Cooking time
20 minutes
Resting time
3 hours

Ingredients
50 g (2 oz/scant ½ cup)
candied orange peel
50 g (2 oz/scant ½ cup) raisins
50 g (2 oz/scant ½ cup)
crushed almonds
1 tbsp Cointreau®
1 tbsp lemon juice
500 g (1 lb 2 oz/4 cups) strong
white (bread) flour
pinch of salt
20 g (¾ oz/1 ⅓ tbsp) fresh
baker's yeast
5 eggs plus 1 yolk, at room
temperature
250 g (9 oz) butter, at room
temperature
50 g (2 oz/scant ¼ cup) caster
(superfine) sugar
Decoration
Icing (confectioners') sugar
Candied fruits (optional)

Specialist equipment
Stand mixer with dough
hook attachment
2 savarin or bundt cake
moulds

- Macerate the candied orange peel, raisins and almonds in a bowl with the Cointreau® and lemon juice.

- Place the flour, salt and yeast in the bowl of a stand mixer fitted with a dough attachment. Switch the mixer on at high speed then add the whole eggs, mixing continuously as you do so. Reduce the speed to medium and mix for 8 minutes.

- Cut the softened butter into small pieces and add to the mix with the caster sugar. Knead for 10 minutes until you have a uniform, elastic dough that comes away from the sides of the bowl.

- Add the dried fruits and the macerating syrup and quickly knead them into the dough to fully incorporate. Cover the bowl with a clean tea (dish) towel and leave to rise for 1 hour at room temperature.

- Knock back the dough to its original volume by hitting it with a spatula or a knife but without kneading it. Set aside in a cool place for 1 hour 30 minutes.

- Preheat the oven to 180°C (350°F/Gas Mark 4).

- Divide the dough equally between 2 savarin or bundt moulds. Leave to prove for 30 minutes, then bake in the preheated oven for 20 minutes, until golden brown and a skewer inserted in the middle comes out clean and dry.

- Remove from the oven and leave to cool in the moulds for 10 minutes before transferring to a wire cooling rack to cool completely. When cool, dust the brioches with icing sugar and decorate with candied fruits, if you like.

Yummy tip

You can also top the brioches with chocolate chips.

Saint Nicolas Brioche Maneles

Makes 40

Preparation time
15 minutes
Cooking time
15–20 minutes
Resting time
1 hour 10 minutes

Ingredients
25 g (¾ oz/1 ½ tbsp) fresh baker's yeast
200 ml (7 fl oz/scant 1 cup) whole (full-fat) milk, warmed
500 g (1 lb 2 oz/4 cups) strong white (bread) flour
100 g (3 ½ oz) butter, at room temperature
100 g (3 ½ oz/scant ½ cup) caster (superfine) sugar
pinch of salt
2 eggs plus 1 yolk
30g (1 oz) melted milk or dark (bittersweet) chocolate

Specialist equipment
Gingerbread man-shaped pastry cutter

- Mix the yeast in 100 ml (3 ½ fl oz/scant ½ cup) of the warmed milk then add 100g (3 ½ oz/generous ¾ cup) of the flour until you obtain a smooth, consistent mixture. Cover with a clean tea (dish) towel and rest for 20 minutes to activate the yeast.

- Melt the butter in a saucepan, add the remaining milk, the sugar and salt. Add the whole eggs and the remaining flour along with the milk, flour and yeast mix. Knead vigorously for about 15 minutes until you have a smooth uniform dough. Cover with a clean tea towel and set aside to rise for 30 minutes.

- Roll out the dough to a thickness of 1 cm (½ inch) on a lightly floured worktop. Use the man-shaped pastry cutter to cut out little men from the dough. Beat the egg yolk in a small bowl and brush it over the dough to glaze. Arrange the dough men on a baking sheet lined with baking parchment, leaving 2 cm (1 inch) between each one to allow for them to spread.

- Preheat the oven to 180°C (350°F/Gas Mark 4).

- Leave the dough to rise for a further 20 minutes, then bake in the preheated oven for 15–20 minutes. Remove from the oven and leave to cool for 5 minutes before transferring to a wire cooling rack to cool completely.

- Using a toothpick dipped in melted chocolate, draw the eyes, mouth, bow tie and shirt buttons on the front of each manele.

Yummy tip

You can also decorate the maneles with royal icing (frosting), see page 24.

Salted Caramel Latte

 Serves 1

 Preparation time
10 minutes
Cooking time
5 minutes

 Ingredients
150 ml (5 fl oz/scant ⅔ cup)
hazelnut (filbert) milk
1 shot of espresso or a double
shot if you prefer a stronger
coffee taste
1 large tbsp salted butter
caramel (optional)
Decoration
Whipped cream
Salted butter caramel
Hazelnut (filbert) pieces

Specialist equipment
Coffee maker or stick
(immersion) blender or
milk frother

- Heat the hazelnut milk in a microwave, small saucepan or, ideally, with the steam wand of a coffee machine. If you have heated the milk using a microwave or saucepan, froth it using a stick blender or milk frother.

- Place a single or double shot of espresso in a glass latte mug. If you do not have a coffee machine, aeropress or cafetière, you can use instant coffee.

- Add the salted butter caramel and the warm frothy hazelnut milk and mix well.

- Decorate the top of the latte with a dome of whipped cream, a swirl of salted butter caramel (if using) and a few hazelnut pieces. Serve hot.

 Yummy tip

Sprinkle the whipped cream with a little cinnamon, if you like, or vary the taste by replacing the hazelnut milk with, for example, almond or oat milk.

Christmas Hot Chocolate

Serves 4

Preparation time
5 minutes
Cooking time
5 minutes

Ingredients
130 g (4 oz) dark (bittersweet)
chocolate
300 ml (10 fl oz/1 ¼ cups)
whole (full-fat) milk
200 ml (7 fl oz/scant 1 cup)
single (light) cream
2 tbsp granulated, Demerara
or brown sugar
1 tbsp vanilla extract
Whipped cream (optional)
Sugar sprinkles (optional)

Specialist equipment
Balloon (wire) whisk

- Finely chop the chocolate, place in a bowl and set aside.

- Pour the milk in a saucepan with the cream, add the sugar and vanilla extract and bring to a boil.

- Remove from the heat as soon as it begins to boil and slowly pour onto the chopped chocolate, stirring well with a balloon whisk until the chocolate has completely melted.

- Pour into 4 glass or ceramic mugs and top with some whipped cream and sugar sprinkles, if you like. Serve hot.

The perfect, warming drink for Christmas Eve!

Yummy tip

Substitute the vanilla for a few drops of peppermint extract, if you prefer.

Chai Latte

Serves 2

Preparation time
10 minutes
Cooking time
5 minutes

Ingredients
6 g (3 tbsp) loose black tea
1 cinnamon stick
1 aniseed star
1 clove
3 green cardamom pods
Grated zest of ½ an orange
250 ml (8 ½ fl oz/1 cup) whole
(full-fat) milk
3 tbsp maple syrup

Specialist equipment
Sugar thermometer
Coffee maker or stick
(immersion) blender or milk
frother

- Put the loose tea in a ball infuser.

- Pour 600 ml (20 fl oz/2 ½ cups) water into a saucepan and heat to 85°C (185°F). Remove from the heat, add the infuser ball or teabag, the spices and orange zest. Leave to steep for 10 minutes.

- Heat the milk with the maple syrup in a microwave, small saucepan or, ideally, with the steam wand of a coffee machine. If you have heated the milk using a microwave or saucepan, froth it using a stick blender or milk frother.

- Pour the tea through a fine-mesh strainer into the hot milk, stir, and serve immediately in glass latte mugs.

A soothing, sweet and aromatic tea.

Yummy tip

For an extra depth of flavour, you can sprinkle over a little ground cinnamon. This recipe also works well using coffee instead of tea.

Christmas Punch

Makes about 1 litre

Preparation time
15 minutes
Resting time
4 days or 12 hours

Ingredients
For the macerated rum
500 ml (17 fl oz/2 cups) good quality rum
80 ml (2 ¾ fl oz/scant 1 ½ cups) sugar cane syrup
1 cinnamon stick
1 star anise
1 clove
1 green cardamom pod
Alternatively use
250 ml (8 ½ fl oz/1 cup) good quality rum
5 tbsp winter spice syrup

Punch de Noël
250 ml (8 ½ fl oz/1 cup) orange juice
250 ml (8 ½ fl oz/1 cup) mango juice
250 ml (8 ½ fl oz/1 cup) pineapple juice
250 ml (8 ½ fl oz/1 cup) passion fruit juice
Grated zest and juice of 1 lime
2 cinnamon sticks
2 aniseed stars
1 vanilla pod (bean)

- If you have time, make the macerated rum 4 days or more in advance. Pour the rum and sugar cane syrup into a bottle and add the spices and seal. Leave to macerate in a dark place for at least 4 days. (You can make this recipe several weeks in advance.)

- After 4 days, taste the rum and adjust the sweetness by adding more sugar cane syrup if it isn't sweet enough. Add more rum if it's too sweet, and leave to macerate for longer if it isn't spicy enough. When the rum is to your liking, remove the spices.

- If you do not have time to macerate the rum, mix 250 ml (8 ½ fl oz/1 cup) rum with the winter spice syrup.

- To make the punch, pour the spiced rum into a large carafe or punch bowl, add the fruit juices, lime zest and juice, the spices and the seeds from the vanilla pod (bean).

- Leave in a cool place for 12 hours before serving.

Recipe Contents

Christmas Truffles 6
Mendiants 8
Marzipan Dates 10
Soft Nougat 12
Dark Chocolate Orangettes 14
Santa's Hat Meringues 16
Melted Snowmen 18
Christmas Stars 20
Christmas Spice Fondant 22
Hanging Heart Biscuits 24
Honey Reindeer Biscuits 26
Speculoos 28
Shortbread Stars 30
Gingerbread Men 32
Christmas Crescents 34
Saint Nicolas' Walking Sticks 36
Little Teddy Bears 38
Vanilla and Chocolate Whirls 40
Jam Shortbread Bauble Biscuits 42
Crinkles 44
Diamonds 46
Christmas Holly Biscuits 48
Christmas Bauble Cupcakes 50
Fir Tree Cupcakes 52
Frozen Nougat with Coulis 54
Snowman Tiramisu 56

Sun Bread with Pink Pralines 58
My Fine Fir Tree 60
Vanilla–Clementine Biscuit Cake 62
Orange Shortbread Crown 64
Merveilleux 66
Gingerbread House 68
Ice Cream Crown with Chestnuts 70
Triple-chocolate Log 72
Lemon and Raspberry Log 74
Vanilla and Caramel Log 76
Chocolate and Raspberry Log 78
Praline and Lemon Log 80
Raspberry and Blueberry Log 82
Mango and Coconut Log 84
Candy Cane with Aniseed 86
Pistachio Crown 88
Gingerbread 90
Stollen 92
Sugared Pretzels 94
Panettone with Candied Fruits 96
Christmas Brioche 98
Saint Nicolas Brioche Maneles 100
Salted Caramel Latte 102
Christmas Hot Chocolate 104
Chai Latte 106
Christmas Punch 108

Acknowledgements

I would like to thank everyone who helped make this book a reality. Thank you to Galatéa and Christine for their confidence. And to everyone at Editions Marabout for all their hard work. Thank you to Sandra Mahut for her patience, her receptiveness, and her lovely photographs!

I dedicate this book to my little imp, FG, my year-round Santa Claus. And thank all of my friends for supporting me and always being there for me.

Please visit me on my website guillaumemarinette.com or on YouTube – you'll have a great time!

Published in 2022 by OH Editions
Part of Welbeck Publishing Group.
Based in London and Sydney.
www.welbeckpublishing.com

First published as *Gateaux de Noel Merveilleux*
© Hachette Livre (Marabout) 2021

Design © 2022 OH Editions

Text © 2022 Guillaume Marinette
Photography © 2022 Sandra Mahut
Translation © 2022 Howard Curtis

A CIP catalogue record for this book is available from the British Library.

ISBN 978-1-91431-769-9

Publisher: Kate Pollard
Editor: Jo Ireson
Designer of UK cover: Studio Noel
Production controller: Jess Brisley
UK cover reproduction: p2d

Printed and bound by RR Donnelly in China

10 9 8 7 6 5 4 3 2 1